Securely Yours: An Agony Aunts' Guide to Surviving Cyber

Amelia Hewitt
&
Rebecca Taylor

ISBN: 978-1-0684454-0-8

DEDICATIONS

For Dan. I love you always. This wouldn't have been possible without your unwavering support and commitment.
For my parents. You empowered me to believe in myself and to dream big. I owe you so much.
Rebecca xxx

For my family, who influenced that empowered little girl who became the woman I am today, and for picking up the thousands of calls I've needed to make it this far.
And for my partner, who has loved me unconditionally, even if my laptop always third wheels us!
Mills xxx

GETTING SUPPORT

We are very proud to share this book with you, but we are conscious that some of the topics relate to mental health and wellbeing. One of the most important messages from this title is that we never want any of you to feel alone. No one should feel like they are just 'surviving', particularly when it does come to periods of mental crisis or trauma.

With that in mind, if you are struggling or need urgent support, please know that the following resources are available to you:

United Kingdom

If you need urgent support, please call 999 or go to your local Accident & Emergency (A&E) department. Alternatively, if you need support during working hours, you can contact your GP for an urgent appointment, if your clinic is open.

Call 116 123 to talk to Samaritans, or email jo@samaritans.org for a reply within 24 hours.

Text 'SHOUT' to 85258 to contact the Shout Crisis Text Line, or text 'YM' if you're under 19.

If you're under 19, you can also call 0800 1111 to talk to Childline. The number will not appear on your phone bill.

Visit the MIND website (https://www.mind.org.uk/information-support/helplines) for helpline advice and immediate guidance.

United States of America

For urgent support call 911, or please go to your local Emergency Room

If you need support during working hours, you can contact your local health centre.

For suicidal thoughts and behaviour dial 988 for the Suicide & Crisis Lifeline. You can also reach them at 1-800-273-TALK (1-800-273-8255).

For mental health issues after a disaster - contact the Disaster Distress Helpline at 1-800-985-5990.

Rest of the World

Whilst we cannot list every resource, your local hospital or medical practitioner are ready to support and help. In addition, you can visit https://www.helpguide.org/find-help where international mental health resources are listed by country.

Please engage. Please get help. When life is a little brighter, this book will be waiting for you.

Sending a little bit of whatever you need,

Rebecca & Amelia

CONTENTS

ACKNOWLEDGMENTS

Primarily, we'd like to thank one another. Writing a book is intense, and writing a book with another person takes a special kind of friendship that can stand the test of late nights, deadlines and cry-laughing in John Lewis' changing rooms (a secret we'll never tell).

All of the contributors, for their time, candour and support. Their efforts in sharing their stories and perspectives have made our lives tenfold easier.

Susie Evershed, and her beautiful brain.

Evangelina Balitskaya, for her fabulous photography skills.

Harry Hewitt, for designing the cover of our dreams.

Jess Hewitt, for her patience and proofing skills.

Callum and Lauren Stott of Matinée Multilingual, for giving us a safe space to shine.

1 WHO'S GOT A SEAT AT THE TABLE?

If you're reading this, chances are you're either considering stepping into the world of cyber, or you're already deep in the trenches. Either way, welcome! This book is designed to be your go-to resource for building a successful career in our industry, while also offering a reminder that you're not alone in this journey. As women in cybersecurity, we've all had our moments, some worthy of a gossip magazine headline, but here's the good news: there's a thriving community of us ready to support you whenever you're ready to connect.

Think of us as your paperback mentors, confidants, and cheerleaders. We've been in your shoes, whether that's feeling overwhelmed by the endless acronyms, unsure about your next move, or just needing reassurance that you belong here. But as every reader of an agony aunt column knows, it takes someone with the right experience to provide guidance, and in order for you to trust us, we'd like you to get to know us.

Rebecca Taylor:

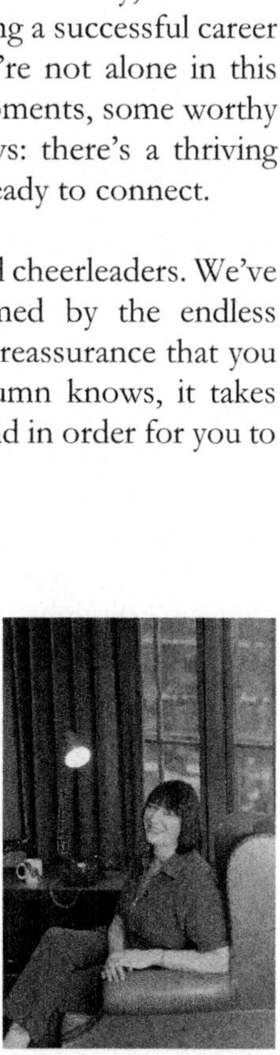

I have always very simply been someone who wanted to help others. I've always wanted to do whatever I could to bring others to the metaphorical table and empower them to shine. I've always wanted to support others in doing what they need to feel happy and safe. Whilst I am starting this section a little back-to-front, this is why I 'do cybersecurity'. It allows me to help people from all walks of life, communities and backgrounds. I can empower individuals to make informed cybersecurity-conscious choices and stay safe online. I can help my colleagues, mentees, and fellow cybersecurity enthusiasts figure out their missions, goals, and cybersecurity aspirations, and get to a point they can own their deserved seat, platform or, cybersecurity status. I can support organisations to best detect, protect, and respond. Helping makes me tick.

When I reflect back, I've always been the helping type. I think it's authentically part of my nature and a leadership style I saw embodied by my first manager, my Dad. During my university years I would work for my Dad, who at the time was an operations manager for a dairy products manufacturer. I would deal with customer enquiries and orders, the emotive calls of older community members panicking because their milk hadn't yet been delivered. Every day I would see the milkmen coming back to the yard and every single one would talk to my Dad. They all cared for him, respected him and trusted him - on one hand he was a direct, clear and strong leader with clear rules. On the other hand, he was always kind, supportive and happy to help. My Dad would jump on a milk float and do a round so one of the staff could take some holiday, celebrate team members successes, but also be there in the darker days of illness and loss. He would be the man who would turn up at your home with a card and some food. He would be the man who would help you to train or to get support if you were struggling. He would offer you a lift home after a cold shift. My Dad just wanted to help. Seeing this from a young age and obviously being blessed with such a bloody awesome father, I knew I too wanted to help and that being that kind of leader is what counted. A person who was compassionate, kind, supportive and wanted to do good, but still knew and could articulate the mission and the motivation. This is why I have got more and more entrenched in the world of cybersecurity - it is the perfect space to live and breathe these attitudes. It is the perfect space to help.

So, to start at the beginning. At heart, I am an English and Creative Writing graduate, but on being released into the 'big bad world' post Uni, I had no idea what to do or where to go. Originally, I remember wanting to be a teacher or a psychologist (some might say I do a little bit of that now!). But anyhow, as I pondered my career, I was headhunted for a role at a cybersecurity firm where they were looking for a Personal Assistant to support the General Manager. I can't say I thought, 'wow, this is my dream job,' but I did know it could be the step on the ladder into a more meaningful role. So, I seized the moment and started in 2014, and I have not looked back since. I have embraced every single opportunity, every chance to shadow and to learn, every opportunity to speak and to project lead, and its lead me to the wonderful role I have today. I have worked in Operations, Project Coordination, Incident Response, Incident Command and now I live in the world of Threat Intelligence. This sounds awesome, right?

My journey however has had personal ups and downs. I have had periods of burnout, of postnatal depression, of the identity crisis that comes with motherhood and career gaps. I have been torn between working and caregiving responsibilities, stifled by self-doubt. Now this list sounds negative, but it's honest and more importantly relatable. In this book I don't intend to dress anything up, but instead share openly. I want you to walk away not only thinking that you can absolutely smash a career in cybersecurity, but that others too have experienced adversity and get how you're feeling, and that ultimately you are not alone. That is my biggest hope, that anyone that reads this knows they will never be alone again.

Day-to-day, my role is a little quirky. In some ways, it's fab because it means I get to enjoy a wealth of different opportunities and interactions, but in other ways, it is a juggle and a priority nightmare. First and foremost, I am Mum to two lovely children, cat-mumma to my beautiful Thumble, and a wife. My family are my everything and I work as hard as I do so I can give them the best possible lives and opportunities. I am all for 'extra-curricular', so on top of my career I am a member of my school Parent Staff Association (PSA) where I volunteer as Secretary. I am also blessed to be a Board Advisor for CybAid (I'll let Amelia give you the details on that fabulous not-for-profit). Finally, I am an active mentor and speaker on the cybersecurity scene - as much as networking is daunting, I love a good conference and more importantly a good natter! I often speak at schools, to girls, and to underrepresented community members looking to succeed in cybersecurity. More recently I have spent time with elders in the community trying to help them to understand cyber threats as they apply to them. On reflection, when I write this it does already sound a lot, but hey ho! I said I liked to help!

Career-wise as I said, my role is in Threat Intelligence (TI) and my goodness I feel lucky. I never would have dreamt I'd end up where I am! Day-to-day my role is split between the joys of knowledge management and human intelligence. On one hand, you'll find me gathering indicators of interest and digging into the 'intelligence weeds' to figure out if we can use it and trust it. You'll find me leveraging as many mechanisms as possible to make sure that intel is useful, actionable and inclusive. On the other hand, you'll find me (or hopefully not!) gathering my findings on access brokerage, data dumps and emerging threats within the realms of the dark web and turning this into my own research. You'll find me monitoring for activities, building my own personas, and distilling new intel out to our researcher team. My role is varied and it is beautiful… and maybe a little busy! Living this career plays to another of my core behaviours - organisation. It is a running joke with my friends on how incredibly organised I am, but seriously - without my giant family calendar, reminders on my Alexa and my day-to-day lists of tasks I would be a lost woman! I need to be organised to live the life I do and thrive in the career I have.

With 2025 here, I finally feel in a position where I have learnt so much, truly understand the risks, dangers and threats that come with being online (and can comfortably explain them), that I genuinely can stop people from falling victim to cybercrime and online harm. This feeling gave me the kick up the bum to finally do my TEDx on safeguarding children's digital footprints, and feeling like I can make a difference. I am delighted you have picked up this book, and as I said I plan to share openly and honestly. I have experienced lots of success, but I have also felt heartbreak, sadness, and loneliness. I have felt different and I have found it hard to own who I authentically am. So, Amelia and I bring you this agony aunt vibe because we get it, and we appreciate how you feel. I've said it once and I'll say it again – You are not alone. Let this book act as inspiration, guidance and a resource to help you glow in the world of cybersecurity. Embrace it, talk to others about it, and if you are having a wobble or need some further advice, know we are at the end of an email, and you can find these details at the end of the book.

Amelia Hewitt:

In drafting this book, the idea of writing over one thousand words about my five-and-a-half-year foray into the world of technology felt overwhelming-do I really have that much to say? Have I achieved enough in that time? Is anyone actually that interested? And really, dear reader, I think that's the whole point of why we need resources like this-I have the confidence to write a book, but describing my time in my own industry makes me want to shrink into a tiny ball. *Interesting.*

Starting with the obvious, I'm Amelia, and my career in cybersecurity didn't start in cybersecurity at all. Having defiantly decided that university wasn't for me, and having never shown an interest in a career in Technology, the natural choice was to embark on a Network Infrastructure apprenticeship for a legal firm-thank goodness for diversity hiring, as told to me by my first manager at said firm within my first month! I can clearly remember the sinking feeling that I had somehow bitten off far more than I could chew, and that I'd never be able to learn the knowledge or skills needed to succeed-and what future did I have? I didn't want to be a network engineer, nor a support analyst forever, I certainly didn't think I fitted the box for one. Besides, all of my apprenticeship cohort were men, and in my mind, this wasn't a role for someone like me. I had dramatically announced several times to my second manager, Minesh, that I was going to leave and that it wasn't for me- thank goodness he was so patient! I've referenced him by name, because I think there are some people who have such a fundamental impact on the professional you become, and he was the first of those people. An effective manager is one who doesn't let you become your own worst enemy, and I knew a thing or two about that as an apprentice! I was also incredibly fortunate to work within a team of men who treated me with so much respect, and welcomed me, despite the fact I was much younger and didn't know the first thing about the Premier League. However, what I lacked in technical skills, I made up for in what I would now consider charm and wit, but at the time was probably a lot of nervous small talk and smiling. Joking aside, I knew early on within my first role that I wasn't going to be within IT forever, but there were two key elements of my role that I absolutely loved - engagement and support.

You see, we pick up a lot of habits from our parents, and having a father in Sales, if I knew one piece of information going into my working life, it was that relationships underpin everything you do. So, whilst I didn't always know which port had what function, nor could I always understand why an angry Lawyer's laptop would constantly freeze (spoiler alert, you can't leave your machine running for six months without a restart), I found that I did quite well. My entire role centred around talking to people, understanding their issues and fixing them- engagement and support. People didn't care if I couldn't immediately fix their issue, because they felt heard, and they felt that I genuinely wanted to support them, regardless of if that was immediate or required some further digging into endless knowledge articles.

The combination of team changes and a pandemic meant that my role had changed dramatically, and having thrived on human connection, supporting from home had turned my job into a chore, rather than a role I genuinely enjoyed. That was, until I was approached to undertake a secondment in the internal Governance team, as part of the wider cybersecurity function. By this time, I had a fantastic manager who was more than willing to support the transition, and I started in my role as a Governance Analyst. Those four months were transformative, and a career in cybersecurity that once felt wildly unrealistic was unfolding in front of me. However, if there's one thing that internal audit lacks, it's the support and engagement factor of my previous role that I'd loved, but I no longer felt that I wanted to go back to working in IT.

On a likely rainy (I live in London) October evening, I was at work drinks with my colleagues, when I happened to be introduced to a man who had transitioned from a military career into Cyber Consultancy. Cyber Consultancy? A concept that was completely foreign to me, but after a few drinks (and a lot of prying), I knew that was it- that was what I was going to do. It had everything, engaging with a variety of people, supporting on solving problems, and I could use my newfound knowledge in cybersecurity. What could possibly go wrong?

Fast forward by a few years, and it was, in fact, all going wrong. The combination of challenging workplace situations, health battles, and a complete loss of self-esteem meant that I was at breaking point. I'd consulted for household names, been commended cross-departmentally, and had excelled beyond the point that I could've ever imagined as a Cyber Consultant, but things could not continue how they were. I was fed up, and exhausted. This is the point in which I must highlight- it is not normal, nor expected to wake up with a pit in your stomach when you think about your working day, and no number of affirmations or payslips will make that go away. For the first time, I handed in my notice with no idea of what was to come next, or how I'd pay my bills.

Armed with a few years of consultancy experience, and the strong belief that if I was going to work in this industry, it was going to be on my terms, I set up Hewitt Partnerships, and started to take on contract work in GRC. This wasn't an overnight fix, and it certainly has challenged me in ways that I didn't anticipate it would, but for the first time in my career, I didn't dread Monday morning. The irony of life is that in my working life up until three months into being freelance, I can honestly say that nothing significant had ever happened to me. That was, until, my dear grandfather very unexpectedly passed away, in the days before my first independent client audit. Navigating supporting my family whilst supporting a client in critical moments of both of their existences is a feeling that cannot be put into words, and what was the lowest moment of my personal life was simultaneously an incredibly high moment professionally, and I wasn't entirely sure how to begin to process this. As anyone who has experienced grief knows, it impacts you profoundly, and I feel as if I could write an entirely different book on grief. However, as a proactive person, I wanted to take the pain I was feeling personally, and channel it into something positive.

As I've touched on before, we learn a lot from those who are around us as we're growing up, and my grandfather personified being the pillar of the community-from working in local government to being on charity boards, his work helped thousands of people, and I wanted to do the same. But delivering GRC work doesn't quite have that impact, even if you are great at it, and thus came CybAid. I wanted to engage with and support those who, like my grandfather, worked tirelessly to help others, but I had a specific skillset, and when looking into it, those organisations needed cybersecurity, but didn't have the budget to have consultancy. So, I set up CybAid, a non-profit committed to offering complimentary cybersecurity consultancy services to industries dedicated to aiding others. At the time of writing, we are close to celebrating our first anniversary, and I couldn't be prouder of the work my team does to bring empowerment to our clients.

It's all been very career-heavy, but I can assure you that I do have fun...sometimes. I'm an avid gym-goer, I will never turn down a restaurant reservation in London, and my social media is a testament to all of the getaways I can cram into a year. With hard work comes (sensible) hard play.

The version of my journey that I have shared so far may paint it out to be mostly without hitch, and if you were to look me up on LinkedIn, you'd also likely think that I have it all figured out with running both a business and a non-profit whilst completing a BSc. However, I want to be transparent, and make it very clear that that whilst I have been incredibly fortunate, and have worked hard to be in this position, it has not been without immense struggle. There was a point in my career that the most talked about detail about me was how I looked, I've been told that my career prospects didn't matter because I potentially want to stay at home once I have a family, and I have been talked down to and passed up on handshakes more times than I can count. The point I'm trying to make, is that even when you look at those who you may think 'have it all', the reality is, being a woman in cybersecurity, even in 2025, can be a whole load of uncomfortable experiences that we're supposed to suck up and be 'grateful' for.

And that's why I'm here.

When two become one (#millennial #ifyouknowyouknow):

It's only natural to wonder how two women with such varying journeys ended up collaborating on a project rooted in raw, unfiltered conversations about an industry we've both loved and loathed in equal measure. The answer lies in a serendipitous (although we both did apply so perhaps not) meeting in the Spring of 2023 during a leadership course designed to empower women in cybersecurity. It was there, amidst discussions of resilience, that we bonded over our experiences-professional triumphs, personal challenges, and the inevitable moments of self-doubt. Later when CybAid was then born, again we became even closer and got to unify on the same cybersecurity cause.

We've spent two years of knowing each other, navigating late-night planning sessions trying to figure out how to run an organisation, and how to make waves in the cybersecurity safety industry (cough cough TEDx Talk). We have indulged in a fair share of gossip, and celebrated each other's victories with genuine enthusiasm, and now we've arrived here ready to impart our wisdom.

Through it all, we've found not only a confidant in each other but also an appreciation for the power of networks and shared experiences. This collaboration is more than just a book, it's a testament to the strength of community, the value of connection, and the lessons learned from navigating a challenging industry.

We want to briefly touch on what to expect in this book. With each chapter, we will provide an overview of the topic at hand, followed by questions. Some of these questions have been made up, but the majority have been asked by mentees and fellow women in industry. We have tried to cover a real expanse of topics, so there should be something for everyone.

We're thrilled to have this opportunity to share our insights with you, and we hope they serve as encouragement, and a reminder that you do belong here, even in the moments when you feel that everything is telling you that you don't.

2 CONVERSATIONS COUNT

In the world of cybersecurity, conversations really do count. Whether it's a chat at an event with a speaker who inspired you, bouncing ideas off a mentor on what to do next or an emergency call with a victim of cybercrime-intentional, meaningful and open conversations are pivotal in shaping your career and next steps. In this chapter we will delve into the power of networking and positive communication, including what it can offer to you and your career.

The Science of Networking-A whistlestop tour

We've had the words 'just network more' thrust upon us since the dawn of our careers, but if you were to ask a handful of professionals, in any sector, what networking actually was, you would likely struggle to get a concise answer. Is it an art? A skill? A science?

When seeking guidance on 'how to network', you can look at endless articles on conversation starters and body language, but understanding the science of networking could be the key to understanding what it actually means to you.

At its heart, networking is deeply rooted in our biology as human beings. We crave connection, and the drive to 'belong' has kept our species from extinction. Our brains have adapted to this need, with our prefrontal cortexes (that govern our social interactions), releasing neurochemicals like oxytocin and dopamine during positive social exchanges.

Oxytocin, the hormone best known when released between romantic partners, new parents with babies, or between lifelong friends, is the hormone responsible for the feeling of being bonded together. It's counterpoint, dopamine, sometimes known as the 'reward' neurochemical, helps us to build habits by giving us positive feelings when a good interaction leads to a positive outcome. Think of it as a reinforcer of good behaviours! When you consider these biological structures, it's hard to imagine why we can't network with the entire world...surely, we are built for it? But on reflection, we all know it isn't that easy.

We're not suggesting that you must form deep connections with everyone you meet - science shows us that it's actually the opposite. To try explain what we mean, and the science behind networking we'll liken it to protecting a network in cybersecurity (cliché, but stick with us).Imagine people as nodes in a network, like devices on the internet. The ties between nodes are the connections or relationships. Groups of tightly connected nodes (you might know it as 'clusters' if you're into networks), are like secure subnets or groups that share common interests. Hold that thought...

A well-known concept in network science (human, not computer), made famous by sociologist Mark Granovetter, is that weaker ties hold more strength than we anticipate. These weaker connections, such as acquaintances, act as bridges between different clusters, giving access to new information and opportunities, much like how connecting to external networks allows the sharing of a wider pool of resources. Protecting and leveraging these 'bridges' can strengthen both our social and digital networks. If we reflect this on to human networks, you don't have to always have deep, meaningful connections with everyone. Sometimes, being an acquaintance and 'touching base' can be enough to get you a foot in a conversation, opportunity, or to make a more useful and tactical relationship with someone else.

So, we understand the biology behind it, and that a varied network of connection types is a good thing, but how do we actually connect with others?

The answer lies in three concepts: trust, influence and reciprocity (with a dash of social proof for good measure). Reciprocity looks to offer value through advice, introductions, or support which can strengthen ties and build goodwill or 'social currency'. Being proactive in your reciprocity signals generosity to others, and goes on to encourage others to share back with you on a deeper level. Similarity and rapport also play their part here, with people gravitating towards those who have similar values, hobbies, or life experiences. This again can go on to create close-knit groups within larger networks, with connected commonalities and like-mindedness, promoting comfort, and ultimately enhancing trust.

It would be misleading to talk about connection without exploring social proof. Our natural instinct as humans to 'seek validation' supports our ability to network. We want others to advocate for us, to sponsor us, and verify our credibility. Social proof amplifies these elements, which allows us to extend our reach across networks. By cultivating a positive reputation and leveraging endorsements or mutual connections, we can increase their influence within our networks, creating bridges to new connections and opportunities.

But how does that translate to the online world? With LinkedIn being a key focal point (and often a source of cringe) of professional networking, we couldn't avoid its presence in modern networking. LinkedIn brings forth the challenge of a digital-first impression, giving us more pressure than reasonable to 'show up' in the best way (and not necessarily the most authentic way). This tied with the many other social platforms we are on, online conferences, and 'virtual lunch and learns', but also real-world connections through social events, cybersecurity experiences, and training course, leaves us really questioning how many relationships we can actually have? How much is too much?

The concept of the digital Dunbar number, introduced by British anthropologist Robin Dunbar, suggests that even in the digital age, our capacity to maintain meaningful relationships remains limited-typically to around 150 people. This modern interpretation of Dunbar's original theory highlights the importance of prioritising quality over quantity in online connections-a mindset that can feel counterintuitive in a world obsessed with collecting contacts.

So now we have walked this whistlestop tour, what do we know? It's not about how many people you know, it's who and what they bring to your life. We can have connections simply for the joy they bring to our lives, but we also have tactical relationships which add value. We will explore this more later, but it's important to also know that strong connections can transform over time into lighter or weaker connections - relationships do not have to last forever. If we relate this to a mentor, it is acceptable to have them in your life whilst they serve the mission or journey you are on, or whilst they can support you or connect you to your next step. It is also acceptable when that mission or vision is accomplished, to step away and keep them as an acquaintance.

Our parting message before we delve into questions: ensure that you are investing the time, energy, and furthermore the trust, influence and reciprocity into the connections and networking opportunities that truly add to your life. This can be the difference between success in the cybersecurity industry, or a much greater struggle. As we've alluded to, it is your network, and therefore, your choice. You can remove people (be it online or in person) from your network if they bring negativity to your life- our industry can feel, at times, like an echo chamber, and that can be exhausting.

The thought of walking into a room and networking terrifies me. I don't know what to do or how to introduce myself. Do you have any tips?

We'll begin by saying that you are not alone in feeling this way. Walking into unchartered territory or simply a space where you feel out of your depth is intimidating. If you cast your mind back to your first day of primary school, or your first day at work, you may have felt nerves, anticipation, or straight-up fear. This is a normal response when facing the unknown.

If we consider the initial fear factor associated with networking out of our comfort zones, a fair chunk of these feelings can be soothed by prior preparation. For example, if you know you're going to an event, you may wish to have a cheeky mooch through LinkedIn or Google to give you some essential context about the event. We've consolidated a list below of some helpful points that may put your mind at ease:

- Your exact route so that you can build a plan and transport options - never fall at that first transport hurdle as the journey itself can often be a source of anxiety.
- The layout of the building or potentially the conference space or room, and also the nearest bathrooms or breakout spaces (it's always good to know where these are, as if you need to step out from nerves, they can be your decompression space). Knowing this kind of detail can help you plan out where you might stand, whether you want to sit or walk around, where you could take someone for a more private conversation.
- LinkedIn can be a source of magic for figuring out who might be going to the same event. Is there someone you know who you could buddy up with? Is there a 'mutual connection' who could facilitate a pre-intro ahead of a physical meeting? Is someone going who you'd simply love to meet?
- Is there an agenda? Will there be any speakers? Is there an event coordinator you can connect with, who can introduce you to some like-minded individuals? Always check out the event page itself and see what information you can gather to make a solid plan.

Research before the event helps you to take ownership for your experience, and in turn, reduce the anxiety associated with networking. You cannot dictate how the conversations will go, or how the people you interact with will react to you, but you can gain an understanding on what can be expected from the event itself by the static details like the agenda, and take comfort from that.

The next thing to consider is how you initially walk into that space and own your voice and platform. You are not at this event or part of this conversation by absolute chance - you are present and attending because you deserve to and because you have something to offer. Again, preparation can really help in you believing this (you'll see a theme here). If you have time before the event, perhaps enroute, grab a notepad, or your notes app, and write answers to the following:

- Why am I going to this event? (P.S. If there isn't authentic reason and instead it's 'because my boss made me', you should be advocating for yourself not to go instead!)
- What do I know about the topics that will be discussed? For example, if it's a networking event about incident response, what 5 things can you comfortably talk to about the world of IR?
- What do you want people to know about you? Are you just a lover of incident response? Are you looking for a mentor? Are you seeking out a new job opportunity? More importantly, are you firm, kind, funny, tired, enthusiastic...?
- What lasting impression do you want to give? What do you want other attendees to have in their minds when they hear your name? Do you want to be known as the 'go-to' for anything? Our experiences have found that by cementing ourselves in a personal brand, people know us for our achievements.

Pondering these questions ahead of a networking event can help you set the boundaries on who you are and what you're willing to share. You could even go as far as to have prebuilt questions and responses - we know plenty of folks who have turned up to networking events with prompter cards to make them feel more comfortable with their conversations.

Know who you are and have faith in that. Whatever method you choose, you should walk into a space feeling comfortable in yourself, and that you have conversation points that you are comfortable with.

Now, we'll put it into practice. You're at an event, and you spot the person you've been looking to connect with, or someone saunters over and says 'Hi I'm Debbie and I work for Acme, who are you?' What will you say? This kind of introduction is where a rehearsed elevator pitch comes into play.

Elevator pitches are brief, clear statements on who you are, what you do, who you do it for, and what you're looking to achieve. They need to be concise, compelling and help you stick in people's minds. This obviously sounds fab, and we're perhaps simplifying it… but if you haven't done an elevator pitch before, this can be blooming tricky! So, our best advice here is to keep it simple. No-one knows you better than you. No-one knows the awesome things you've accomplished more than you. No one knows what you want better than you do. It doesn't need to be bold or brash, it doesn't have to be a huge dream of defeating all cybersecurity evils, or equally so small that it is almost meaningless. It just has to be authentically you. Say it how it is and own it. Then, practice makes perfect, so keep refining that elevator pitch, until it's a statement you are proud to say.

There's a formula for elevator pitches that we've found useful:

1. Who are you?
2. What do you do?
3. Who do you do it for?
4. Why are you here? Or what would you like to achieve?

Finally, a point that cannot be avoided, and one that we know causes stress when it comes to networking. Walking into a space (virtual or not), and there being nobody who looks or feels like you. For us as writers, an example could be when walking into a cybersecurity conference and being met by a sea of men. It's uncomfortable, isolating and intimidating-and incredibly common! Whilst we all continue to strive for representation in the cybersecurity field, it is still a very obvious issue. We do not have a solution for this nor do we want to diminish how anyone feels when it comes to feeling like the 'odd one out' or the 'different' one. All we can say is to be proud that you had the guts to walk into the space, to be proud of your individuality. Those around you will be lucky to get the diversity of thought, experience and conversation that you bring by being the one who is 'different' to the norm. That is a feeling that only you can muster and take ownership of, but one we believe and advocate for.

What kinds of questions should I ask when networking?

Networking can come in all shapes and sizes. On one hand, it could be small talk, but we believe that networking when used in the right way, should always be intentional.

At a high-level, you might wish to ask broader, less personal questions. Think of them as a method to get a foot in the door. This may consist of 'warmer-uppers', where you ask if they've seen the latest in the world of cybersecurity news, or talk about a shared industry experience (e.g. 'Have you been impacted by the recent change to XYZ Compliance Policy?') These broader questions can bring reassurance to both you and the other person through common ground - one of the easiest methods of building trust.

However, we consider the real purpose of networking to be forming meaningful (and beneficial) relationships with the right kinds of people. In some cases, you may start with a broad question, and actually realise that the individual isn't quite what you expected them to be. But fear not, they may leverage their own network to connect you to someone more aligned. It is perfectly natural to work the room, mingle, as it were, and figure out who you want to have more intentional and meaningful conversations with. We'd encourage you to remember names and faces, and where you can, work quickly. For some people, this can be challenging. If you struggle with remembering names, try repeating the name immediately after hearing it or making a mental connection to their workplace or role. Associating the name with something relevant to your conversation can also help to reinforce memory.

If you are seeking a meaningful connection, it is important to make a conscious effort to get to know someone on a deeper level. Connections need to be nurtured and treated in a way that fosters trust, influence, and reciprocity. We've got a few tricks to help you to do this:

- Always ask questions on topics that you're genuinely interested in-you can always tell when you're talking to someone who's disengaged, so others will know too.
- Ask 'open' questions. This may be as simple as asking a question that requires further elaboration, rather than a simple 'yes' or 'no' answer, and consider where you could ask follow-up questions. A closed question closes the chat.
- Actively listen and respond to their answers. Showing that you are absorbing what they say by interacting with their response builds familiarity, and therefore trust. For a bonus point, refer back to their previous answers in your later conversations.

- And most importantly… get to the point! Once you've asked those foundational 'nice to know' questions, progress to the topics that you really want to venture into, instead of staying in the broad peripherals. If the conversation is going well, go for it, and ask what you want to know!

Now if you're embracing the above and loving the connections, it is important to remember two other key factors. First off, remember to keep on track with your questions - avoid getting too personal or emotive. Particularly if you are setting the foundations of a future relationship, you don't want to make the individual feel uncomfortable or under pressure to discuss non-cybersecurity topics. You also don't want to drag them into unnecessarily triggering conversations, a good example being political opinions or views on differing geopolitical situations. Trust us, if it's a good connection, the personal side and the 'meatier' chats will come in time. Secondly, keep checking the energy of the room and environment. Is it the right time to be networking? Are you engaging in the right topics and conversations? Should you be dipping out to have a more private conversation as opposed to talking to a group? Are you being conscious to the moment and that person's time? All things to consider when you are loving the networking energy!

This being said; we hold our hands up and admit that we have dodged the original question of what you could actually ask when networking. Unfortunately, these questions do have to be guided by your actual conversation and personal networking mission, however, we do want to share some initial questions shared and created by 'Elegant Mind' that could help if you aren't feeling as confident yet with 'going with the flow'.

The following questions are fantastic at getting those interactions going and could be memorised or jotted on a cue card to help you own your voice:

- What makes you most excited these days in the world of cybersecurity?
- What motivated you to get into cybersecurity?
- What do you see as the coming challenges and opportunities in cybersecurity?
- What/who has been the biggest influence in your career?
- What does your typical work day look like?
- What is your most valuable skill?
- What would you have done differently in your career if you could go back?
- What positive habits have you adopted for success?
- What is a recent achievement which made you proud?
- What is your current professional goal?
- How can I help you meet your goals?

- What is the single most important action which has changed your career?

Networking is not just a professional buzzword; it's an opportunity for your personal growth. By understanding the science behind our interactions and embracing both the depth and breadth of our relationships, we can build networks that not only advance our careers, but bring us a bit more joy within them. Remember, it's not about collecting contacts; it's about cultivating connections that matter.

What kinds of individuals should I look to have as part of my network? Are there any key positions I should be looking to fill?

Your network should be made of individuals that enrich not just your career, but also your life, because despite what the hustle culture tell us, you can actually enjoy your career too. Your network can help you to find new opportunities, areas for development, and safe spaces to experience the highs and lows that accompany a career in cybersecurity.

Having a network is a gift.

With that in mind, your network should include people that enable you to feel that you can shine-those who bring you comfort. Just because your colleague is connected to someone, it doesn't mean you have to be too. Your network is your own to evolve and enhance over the span of your career.

Two characters (at a minimum) that should be in your network are a mentor and a sponsor. Both add significant value to your brand, profile, experience and opportunities, but often in different ways.

Mentors are sounding boards and trusted advisors who you can bounce ideas off of. Be it an upcoming promotion or planning for the future, mentors are your personal counsel, on hand to support with career steps. Mentors share their experiences and professional knowledge in the form of advice, and also act as a bridge to their own networks. Neither of us are shy in saying how transformational mentors have been in introducing us to influential individuals, offering career advice, or even providing guidance around CVs. It's important to know that the number of mentors you can have is unlimited. Whilst that sounds exciting, we don't mean to treat mentorship like an 'all you can eat buffet'! Limiting your mentors to those who can support in specific areas is an advisable boundary. We recommend having one internal mentor to the organisation you are in (if working) and one external. This allows you to have the support of someone 'in the know' when it comes to how your teams, tools and management structures work, but that you can also benefit from the voice of someone external who hasn't been influenced by your own organisational politics. It is also key to note that a mentor does not necessarily need to model the career you have, or want. That person may embody values that you appreciate, or have found success in their own field, but a mentor isn't always a role model, rather a supporting perspective.

Sponsors are a little different. A mentor provides advice and gives feedback, whereas a sponsor is an advocate. A sponsor represents you, is your voice in 'the room', and tries to source you opportunities to get you a seat at the table. They are far more proactive, and more invested in your ability, potential and personal development. Again, we have both benefited from brilliant sponsors who have thrown our name in the mix for training opportunities, chances to travel, and even promotions. Sponsors are longer term commitments and represent one of the most meaningful career relationships you can have. Mentors come and go as you grow (much like the flings of your teenage years), but sponsors can fundamentally be a relationship for life.

As advocates for these relationships, it would be negligent of us to encourage you to find these connections without suggesting how you could go about sourcing your own. Usually, a mentor is someone you already know, however, we are seeing more programs that pair strangers, and some of our industry friends have found theirs via LinkedIn-the choice is yours. Having a pre-established relationship with a person can make the mentoring conversation smoother. Either way, when reaching out to a potential mentor, start with curiosity and respect. A genuine connection is built on mutual trust and shared understanding, so approach them with thoughtful questions and a clear idea of what you're hoping to learn. It's also key to remember that mentorship is a relationship, not a transaction, so you must reciprocate in opening up and sharing your perspective.

Unlike mentors, sponsors often seek you out because they see potential in you within your organisation. That said, you can position yourself for sponsorship by demonstrating excellence in your work and building relationships with those in leadership positions.

That said, you can approach a sponsor. When approaching someone as a potential sponsor, the key is to showcase what you bring to the table. Highlight your achievements, both within your work and any extra-curricular work you've done within the industry, share your aspirations, and make it clear how their support could make a difference. Sponsorship relationships are often slower to build, and more organic, so you may need to be patient and focus first on building rapport.

That's our view on what a network should be made up of positive relationships, mentors and a sponsor!

How can I best network if I find these forms of social interaction challenging?

We've said 'we've been there' plenty of times already, but if there is one question we can both relate on, it's this one. Social interaction can be awkward, even for the most confident person. We aren't all wired the same way, and what may feel comfortable in a neurotypical brain may not resonate the same with a neurodivergent one.

Redefining how you see networking can take away the pressure that can often lead to the challenging emotions surrounding it. It's important to remember that networking doesn't have to look like a room of one hundred people, it may be as small as an online connection, or talking to one person. You don't have to dive into conferences right away. Begin with one-on-one interactions in low-pressure settings. Reach out to colleagues, or people in your field for a quick coffee chat or virtual meeting. If in-person interactions feel overwhelming, start with online platforms as an alternative. This doesn't even need to be a direct message, it could just be a comment or a re-share, or someone else's content, and build connections from there. This allows you to network at your own pace, from the comfort of your chosen environment.

We're lovers of preparation, and it can also help if you find networking to be challenging. Before reaching out via direct message or attending a networking event, research the topics that are likely to be discussed. Have a few questions or conversation starters ready. For example:

- 'I noticed you worked on (specific project). I'd like to hear more about how you approached it.'
- 'I've been exploring (specific topic), and I'd love to hear your perspective on it.'

If you're better at writing than speaking, focus on considered emails or messages. If you're more comfortable in structured interactions, attend workshops or webinars where networking often happens naturally.

Once you've found your preference, don't forget to follow-up. Sending a thank-you message, or sending them an article related to their field builds consistency, and that yields fantastic results.

Our overarching message is to be kind to yourself-for a lot of us, the start of our careers may be the first time we ever have to interface with so many new individuals, and that can be overwhelming. Networking is a skill, not an innate trait. Like any skill, it improves with practice. Make sure to set realistic expectations for yourself and celebrate small wins, and over time, it won't feel quite so challenging.

I have a connection, who knows someone else that I'd love to get to know. How best can I ask for an introduction?

Expanding your network doesn't always mean that you have to seek out new connections, and we've personally seen the benefits of sharing networks with others. Understandably, it can be a tricky thing to broach, even if you know the person you're asking very well, so we can offer some guidance on making this slightly less anxiety-inducing!

Firstly, you need to be on good terms with the connection that you're going to ask-this probably goes without saying! You don't necessarily have to know them well, but having rapport means that they feel comfortable to potentially talk or even advocate on your behalf. When asking, it's important to be clear on why you'd like to connect with the other person. It could be to ask for professional advice, collaboration, or even to discuss a shared interest - Whatever the reason, be upfront. You may even want to make the introduction yourself, referencing your mutual connection, rather than your connection doing it for you. If you do choose to go down this path, clarify with the connection before any intros are made, and make sure you have their consent to 'name-drop'.

We have found when asking for a favour of this type, it can flow more naturally when conducted over a coffee or a call. You might however wish to do this via a message or email, depending on the circumstances. We've put together a sample of how you might ask for an introduction, if you're planning on doing this in writing:

'Hi [Connection's Name],

I hope this message finds you well! I noticed that you know [Person's Name], and I've been really impressed by their work in [specific area]. I'd love the opportunity to connect with them to [reason, e.g., learn more about their insights on X or explore potential collaborations].

Would you feel comfortable introducing me please? I'd be happy to provide a brief message if that makes it easier for you, or reach out to them myself and let them know of our connection. Please don't hesitate to let me know if this isn't feasible, and thank you in advance for considering it!'

See? It doesn't need to be lengthy, or awkward, and you'd be surprised by how open, especially in our industry, people are in sharing connections. The worst they can say…is no. And besides, there's a whole sea of professionals to connect with, so if it doesn't work out, you've not lost anything! Approaching these requests with confidence and respect will be your biggest ally.

Chapter 2 - Closing Words

What a chapter, right? We will end as we began...conversations really do count. They may come in a variety of formats; they can be high level and casual, or deeply meaningful and passionate. Consider what you're looking for as you engage and do your preparation before any opportunities that could be integral to your development, or with an individual you'd like to build a relationship with.

Your network must suit you, your objectives and your vision. It should be a guarded, respected collection of individuals who empower you to be your greatest self, so don't just let anyone waltz in!

Finally, connections will come and go, but be sure as part of that journey to have a flurry of mentors, and your own advocates or sponsors for each step in your career. Networking and positive communication are powerful - own them!

3 IN THE FACE OF PERSONAL ADVERSITY

According to the Cambridge Dictionary, a challenge is '(the situation of being faced with) something that needs great mental or physical effort in order to be done successfully and therefore tests a person's ability'. We think it's fair to say most people face their share of challenges, some openly, and some privately- albeit some challenges being more difficult than others! Challenges can appear at anytime, anywhere, and to anyone, but we all typically manage to overcome them and move on to the next. Challenges can often be something we choose to face on, or avoid until they become significant, and potentially debilitating.

Adversity is synonymous with challenge, with most of us facing some kind of adversity in our lifetimes. It could as an example be the loss of a loved one, or a big life change. Adversity is a situation you have no choice but to face, even when every fibre of your being wants to run and hide! It can be painful, soul-destroying, limiting. For some, adversity can be the final hurdle of a long road of challenges, and they choose to walk away. For others, adversity is the trigger, to identify the challenge and therefore the next step in taking positive action to enact change. Adversity often has this 'sunny-side up' light shone against it ('she fought in the face of adversity'), when actually, adversity is an event or situation which can fundamentally stop someone in their journey to success.

Adversity often needs time to brew, before the challenges within it can be identified and tackled. In your working life, you will come across adversity, it's inevitable as we go through the trials and tribulations of surviving the modern world, and so we hope we can shed some light on our experiences of adversity, and how we've 'made it work'.

One final note to make - we have both faced different adversities during our cybersecurity careers. In the Q&A part of this next section, we are going to be even more open and honest than we have already, and on occasion respond to your questions as individual writers. The questions themselves resonated with us both in different ways and so it felt best to split them up based on what we could authentically relate to and share lived experiences and responses to.

How can I balance my health and well-being whilst climbing the career ladder?

I (Amelia) have largely chosen to keep my personal life, particularly my health, separate from my professional life unless absolutely necessary. That said, when we planned this section, I felt a pang of guilt. If I wasn't honest, someone out there who might be feeling as I have felt in the past year might miss the chance to know that it is possible to juggle two contending lifestyles-being chronically unwell whilst climbing the career ladder.

I don't share my experience for pity. I am incredibly privileged, unlike many women, that my health concerns were taken seriously by my GP and treated years earlier than many others. Yet, no amount of gratitude can erase the immense stress of being unwell at such a crucial point of my professional development.

For years, I dismissed my symptoms as stress or poor lifestyle choices. In 2023, after a particularly challenging period (it's 2025 and if we can't talk about periods here, I've lost all hope) landed me in A&E, I reluctantly visited my GP. Months of scans, unsettling blood tests, and difficult conversations about my fertility later, I was diagnosed with Endometriosis in 2024. This condition affects an estimated 176 million women worldwide, around 1 in 10 in the UK alone. If you don't know a woman with Endometriosis, now you do!

Sadly, as you may have experienced, women's health in the UK is poorly managed. Over 750,000 women are currently awaiting Gynaecology services, a staggering number that I've struggled to comprehend. Having likely spent years managing symptoms, I've become adept at 'grinning and bearing it.' But Endometriosis isn't just 'a bad period.' It's an array of debilitating symptoms that drain you constantly. For me, the condition progressed rapidly, leaving surgery as my only viable option to feel any kind of relief. I underwent surgery in November 2024, which was impressively quick given the usual waiting lists, and it has been the biggest challenge I have ever faced, both physically and mentally.

What I want to emphasise is that during this time: before surgery, during recovery, and even now as I navigate long-term management, I ran a business, pursued a degree, and maintained CybAid. And let me tell you, it was incredibly hard, hard enough that I'd feel inclined to call it f***ing hard. You wouldn't know from the smiling LinkedIn posts or the amount of work I was taking on that I felt as if my body was completely failing me, and that in turn, I was going to have to give up on a career I'd worked so hard for. That's why I feel equipped to offer advice on managing these challenges.

I truly believe that balancing your health and well-being with career progression starts with building on your self-awareness. You need to understand your limits and recognise what your body and your mind needs. It's tempting to push through pain or exhaustion, but if you're trying to do that all of the time, you're going to break yourself. I remember one of my wonderful friends, who was my manager at the time, telling me that not every day was going to be a great work day, and nobody expected it to be, and I have always remembered that. If you're having a bad day, it's okay to reschedule that meeting or delegate a task. Taking care of yourself isn't a sign of weakness, and you shouldn't see it that way-it's a strategy for sustainability.

I would call my first section of advice, the 'fluffy' bits, because realistically, you can be as kind to yourself as you want, but the environment around you, be that your workplace or education institution, will have a considerable impact on your ability to manage health with a blossoming career. The most practical advice that I can give is to be transparent. Open up to trusted colleagues or managers about your situation if you feel comfortable doing so. I've found that transparency, when approached thoughtfully, often leads to accommodations that make balancing work and health more manageable. For example, I've had to attend a lot of appointments, often taking chunks out of my working day, but because I'm open with my clients, they trust that I will complete my tasks, but with the flexibility that it won't necessarily be during working hours. I've also found that when I talk to others in the workplace about my condition, they open up about how similar issues have impacted them, and it has made space for such meaningful connections and understanding without intentionally doing so.

Time management is another critical tool, and it ties in well to self-awareness. Use your energy wisely by focusing on high-impact tasks when you feel most capable. For me, this fluctuates based on my hormones. Sometimes, mornings are when I'm most productive, so I schedule my most demanding work then and save less intensive tasks for later in the day when I may be more tired. Hand-in-hand with time management is establishing boundaries. Making it clear to colleagues or clients that you are unavailable or only have a specific amount of time or capacity due to a health factor can be pivotal in helping you to manage the balance. I find that blocking my calendar with the tasks that I'm doing to keep myself free from becoming overloaded with meetings or overwhelmed with my workload has been a fantastic way, especially whilst I recover, to set time-managed boundaries on my working life, so that my time is protected, which in turn, enables me to rest in my down-time.

And potentially most crucially, take the time to invest in activities that restore your energy and bring a sense of joy and balance to your life. The reality of living with a chronic condition, in my experience, is that it comes with both a lot of grief, and sadness. These moments of self-care are essential for maintaining your overall well-being, whilst giving yourself time that isn't required to be 'productive'-you're doing enough as it is. Despite being in physical pain, the gym has become a lifeline for me, and I'm incredibly fortunate to work with the most wonderful Personal Trainer, Jemma, who has seen both my professional bests and my healthcare nightmares, and is always agile in how we can make it work for me on that particular day. We talked about a network, and your 'village' to sustain a healthy working life isn't always about your colleagues, it's those who enable you to show up as your healthiest, happiest self.

I personally want you to remember that prioritising your health and well-being is not a distraction or obstacle to your professional success. Instead, it is the foundation upon which sustainable achievement is built. By owning self-awareness in your way of life, implementing practical methods of creating a flexible working life and making restorative practices a regular part of your routine, you're not just enduring the challenges of the day-to-day; you're equipping yourself with the energy, focus, and positivity needed to thrive in navigating both mountains. You are not defined by your career, or your health, rather a tricky amalgamation of how you choose to balance and approach these situations.

Looking towards the future, I will potentially have a long road ahead of condition management, and fertility struggle, topics I never thought I'd feel comfortable discussing publicly. However, in the course of being more open about my illness, I have spoken to so many women (and men) who have been exactly where I am now, and have prevailed against those uncertain odds. So please, let me be the example, to you, that if you are going through a health battle that leaves you feeling isolated, and scared for the future of yourself and your career, that it does get rosier. It doesn't mean it'll be easy, but you will become stronger than you could even imagine, and you'll 'make it work'-because that's what we do, as women.

How can I best juggle having a career in cybersecurity and being pregnant/a mum?

If you've been reading right from the beginning, you'll know that I (Rebecca) am a very proud mumma bear, so when I saw this question, I jumped at it. I have had to play the game of juggling my cybersecurity career alongside pregnancy/young children and it really isn't easy.

Sadly, there are lots of statistics out there which highlight that motherhood and a cybersecurity profession is not as compatible as it should be. I am blessed to be friends with a fabulous lady called Sophie Creese (go check her out!) who runs an organisation called MotherBoard. In January 2024, in collaboration with HeyFlow, MotherBoard launched the 'The Reality of Mums in Tech' project where they surveyed a bunch of mums from the industry to try and get a real understanding of what was going on in the space. When the findings were announced I was really quite disappointed but in a strange kind of way affirmed when I think about the experiences of many of my counterparts.

According to their report:

- 40% of respondents felt like their career was held back during their pregnancy
- 39% who were on track for promotion ahead of their pregnancy have been promoted since
- 47% feel less valued after they have returned to work
- 58% have considered leaving their role since returning to work
- 54% feel like their career has been held back due to having children

These statistics crush me. I find it really hard to accept that this is the industry I am in.

I am one of what feels like a small number, who had a positive experience when transitioning into being a mum and holding on to what has been the career I've wanted. It hasn't been without issue - I openly hold my hands up and say that I had a messy pregnancy with lots of hospital stays for hyperemesis and very high blood pressure. I had what I would describe as traumatic birthing experiences which did tie into me having postnatal depression. I would also say that as babies, neither of my children were very lucky in terms of health. It was rough. It was tough. I had to dig deep. I had to do what I could, when I could and accept my career pauses, that I had to let things drop if I was going to survive. I had to accept I couldn't do everything. But when I did come back and I was working, my employer understood my needs (driven by my transparency), and still to this day are the flexible, considerate organisation I need to be successful. Maybe I'm lucky, maybe it's the way I handled it (more on that shortly).

I have however spoken to my fair share of mentees and supported fellow mothers through some pretty horrific workplace experiences as a result of pregnancy and motherhood. The statistics from MotherBoard do ring true. cybersecurity as an industry and a vast percentage of organisations that live within it, need to do so much more to empower women to be successful whatever caregiving, fertility or reproductive process (e.g. menopause) they are going through. I will stop ranting now, but it does genuinely make me angry that so many people are leaving, and in too many cases not even joining the industry because one way or another they think there isn't a space for them.

So, to the advice! When I drill down, be a successful juggler has really come down to these points:

Knowing what I was entitled to.

What did work have to offer me? Where did I legally stand? What could the NHS/Local Government/supporting agencies offer me so I could be a mum and work successfully? I took the time to understand what the childcare situation was in my area and took the time to visit nurseries and sign up to waiting lists. Having a full picture with what was available allowed me to plan, evaluate my situation with facts as opposed to hormones and feelings, and make informed choices.

By leveraging the tools and policies my organisation offered to help me feel happy and in control.

Think reasonable adjustments and tweaks to my working environment to suit not only my changing body but my changing life – for me this came in the form of remote working, a better chair to support my back and a pedestal. If I hadn't done my research, I'd probably have missed these options and comforts.

Taking the time to talk to HR and understand our organisational policies were a gamechanger for me. Simply understanding what the policies for maternity leave, parental leave, and sick leave actually looked like helped. Again, it allowed me to make informed choices at different stages of my life and not have to instead make mistakes at work or ill-informed career choices because of trying to juggle too much in times of struggle.

Surrounded myself with people who could support me and raise me up.

Pregnancy can be lonely. Having a newborn can be lonely. My son was a 'covid baby' so trust me I get it. Which is why I cannot stress enough why people you trust around you that can drop you some shopping in, that you can have a moan to, or can cover something at work on your behalf, genuinely makes a difference. They have to be individuals you trust and that are happy to be 'your person', but they are out there just waiting for you to ask. My support group considered of my mum and mother-in-law, a close friend at work, my therapist and my GP. Together they make my juggle manageable.

Document everything! Have a career development plan, have a training plan, have documented goals!

When you are sleep deprived, you smell a bit funky, your small person is screaming in your face, and you haven't been at work for three months, it can be bloody hard to remember career goals, let alone who you even are! This is why it's important to keep a track of what you are working towards and what the bigger vision is. Timeframes may change, as your life changes so may the vision itself, but have a plan and make sure that is accessibly documented and articulated to your leadership.

Every opportunity I could I reaffirmed to my leader what I wanted. I significantly ramped up our check in's. I ensured that at any given time I had a career development plan to explain what I wanted and needed.

And finally, I held my leadership accountable as I transitioned into motherhood and beyond.

So, if you've done number four, then it's in your hands to keep waving the flag for your career dreams and aspirations. You may be out on maternity leave, but if your manager clearly knows what you want for your career, they should be able to advocate for you should a role or opportunity come up. With that in mind, making sure your leader is there and prepped for any 'Return to work' days, that they have an agenda and a plan particularly for when you do come back, but also that as you do get back into the swing of work you have regular check ins on what is happening and if your role still fits with what you need and what you want from your career... it all counts.

Whilst these points are great to call out, you need to be able to advocate for yourself and not only say what you need, but say when you're not receiving something you should be. Whilst it can be intimidating to call HR or to have a challenging conversation with a manager, you have to be incredibly matter of fact – a lot of what I have spoken about is an entitlement or is driven by documented policies and procedures. They owe you, so claim it. In terms of finding like-minded people and support networks, I lost count of the amount of mother and baby classes, mother meet ups, pregnancy support classes, newborn support groups available in my local area but also online. Do your research and find a space where you feel safe and can make meaningful connections with people who can support you. You do not have to be alone. It only takes you to have one good friend or relationship and the load can be that bit lighter and the days that little bit brighter.

Whilst having children can mean a 'career pause', and returning to work post children can be a juggle, it doesn't mean you stop having a voice, work ethic or career goals and aspirations. You deserve to shine and to be successful on your own terms. Having a child and wanting a career, you really need to drive and decide exactly what those terms look and feel like and stick to them. But I promise you, you can have a career in cybersecurity and be a mum. I can't dress up the juggle, but harnessing the five points I mentioned will help.

I'll end with the final and most important point in 'making it all happen' - That is to be kind to yourself. As a mum, I still beat myself up about working and not being there for the kids 100% of the time. I worry that they see me at my laptop, but I know if I wasn't that my daughter couldn't do her singing classes, and my son wouldn't own such an unnecessary amount of Optimus Prime toys (if you know, you know). I feel sad when it's half term, I'm on a conference call and I've had to chuck snacks at them so they are quiet. It happens... It is ok. Many of us mums (and dads) are doing 'the juggle' - know that you aren't alone but that also as your children grow, your career will continue to change, evolve and move on. The juggle is just the 'rite of passage' to get there.

I feel like I am on the brink of burnout. I am pushing so hard in both my personal and professional life, but I'm not sure I can carry on. Can you help?

Burnout is a topic we've seen absolutely soar post-pandemic, and as unfortunate as it is that it's becoming increasingly common, we're finally seeing proper discourse in the media around how we can spot and prevent burnout in our own lives. For those of you who have never heard of it, burnout can be described as a state of physical, mental, and emotional exhaustion that's caused by chronic stress. There isn't an official diagnosis or medical condition, but it is a very real experience that can affect your ability to work and maintain relationships. We see burnout in varying environments, including the workplace, education, and in personal spaces such as parenthood or during significant life changes. 91% of adults in the UK reported to Mental Health UK in 2024 that they had experienced high or extreme levels of pressure or stress within the last year, and this is exactly what leads to a burnt-out workforce.

Burnout and stress are closely related but not the same. Stress is typically short-term and while it may affect your sleep, energy, and emotions, you can usually still engage with the tasks causing the stress. Burnout, on the other hand, leaves you feeling deeply detached and demotivated to the point where it disrupts your ability to function and even to feel hope. In the workplace, this may be caused by prolonged periods of high-stress without adequate down-time to recuperate and regulate your nervous system.

So, how do you know if you're approaching burnout? Burnout develops gradually over time and can often go unnoticed or misdiagnosed as stress or anxiety. Most people experience a mix of symptoms, from extreme exhaustion, to disconnection from others. When identifying burnout in others, it is often reflected in their behaviour both at work and at home. Mental Health UK breaks down the symptoms of burnout into three categories: physical, emotional and behavioural. For the purpose of giving you the most accurate information, we've summarised their fantastic guidance below on the signs of burnout:

Burnout often manifests physically, with common signs including persistent exhaustion and recurring sleep disturbances, such as insomnia. Physical discomfort like frequent headaches, muscle or joint pain, and gastrointestinal issues, such as nausea or loss of appetite, are also typical. People experiencing burnout may notice weakened immunity, leading to frequent illnesses, as well as high blood pressure or difficulty breathing.

Emotionally, burnout can lead to feelings of helplessness, self-doubt, and worthlessness. Individuals may feel trapped, overwhelmed or detached, often experiencing a lack of motivation, a cynical or negative outlook, and a diminished sense of satisfaction or achievement. Burnout can also result in a loss of interest in previously enjoyable activities and persistent feelings of dread, worry or anxiety.

Burnout is also evident in behaviour, with procrastination, difficulty concentrating, and decreased productivity being common signs. This can often be one of the key signs we can pick up on from a team-mate or employee perspective. Affected individuals may isolate themselves from others, withdraw from responsibilities, or rely on food, drugs or alcohol as coping mechanisms. They may also become irritable, prone to outbursts, and take frustrations out on others. Increased tardiness or absenteeism, especially in professional settings can also indicate burnout.

With 49% of respondents to Mental Health UK reporting that their employer doesn't have a plan to spot the signs of chronic stress, it is becoming increasingly important to have a personal plan in place to manage burnout, ideally before it creeps in. However, if you are an employer, or a manager, we've collated some advice in supporting your teams to prevent burnout. It is a team effort.

- Encourage your team members to respect holiday time and avoid working excessive overtime in order to establish boundaries between work and personal time. Provide flexible work options, such remote work or rearranged schedules, to assist in successfully juggling their personal and professional obligations.
- Establish an environment where your team may talk about their difficulties without worrying about being judged. Check in with how your team are feeling on a regular basis to spot stress early and give them access and encourage them to use to tools like wellness programs and employee assistance tools.
- Workloads should be reasonable and in line with the responsibilities and abilities of team members. Encourage fair goal-setting, refrain from overburdening employees, and divide duties equally to keep people from feeling overburdened.
- Recognise and celebrate team members' accomplishments on a regular basis, no matter how minor. Expressing gratitude for their efforts encourages drive and a sense of worth, which helps avoid alienation and disengagement.
- Encourage your organisation to offer management training on how to spot early indicators of burnout and be given tools to help their teams. Additionally, provide team members with career advancement and skill development opportunities to foster long-term engagement and a feeling

of purpose.

At this stage, we've explored what burnout is, how we can spot it in ourselves (and in our peers), and how you may wish to combat burnout in your own organisation if you have the authority to implement change. But, how can you prevent burnout at an individual level?

Much of what we're going to tell you in avoiding burnout will sound similar to other sections of this book, but these themes are intrinsically linked, and you'll also find that by implementing a few core strategies to protect your emotional wellbeing, you'll also be preventing burnout.

Our first, and arguably the most important piece of advice that we can give, is to set boundaries. This came up earlier in this section, so we won't 'bang on' too much, but being adept at boundary setting will absolutely change your life. In practice, this might look like defining your working hours, and sticking to them-we work in cybersecurity, not an emergency department, and unless there's a major incident declared…that task can probably wait until tomorrow. Additionally, this might also look like taking your assigned breaks, and using that time to do something that disconnects you from your working life, such as exercise or going for some time outdoors. You may also wish to adopt some of our earlier recommendations, such as calendar blocking, or removing your work applications from devices that could disturb you in your personal time.

With that in mind, how you spend your time outside of work defines a large portion of how you 'turn up' in the workplace. Take some time to consider how you are spending the time that isn't spent working. Are you finishing work and collapsing on to the sofa for hours, eating foods that are fast but not nourishing, and keeping your socialising limited to social media? In order to prevent burnout, create a lifestyle that enriches you. We understand that this is easier said than done, and with responsibilities like children and caring for relatives, this may not be as simple. But as a guideline, consider having three types of 'hobbies' (we use hobbies lightly, as these may be interchangeable activities that you have within your routine):

1. A hobby that keeps you active: consider physical activities that promote your health and well-being. We're not telling you to run a marathon (unless that's your thing), but find something active that brings you those endorphins! That could be something gentle, such as Pilates, or even something as easy as grabbing a coffee and going for a stroll. Perhaps you want something higher intensity like HIT classes, or spin classes. Whatever gets you moving, is a great contributor to preventing burnout.
2. A hobby that keeps you creative: explore activities that stimulate your imagination and allow self-expression. You may roll your eyes at this one,

as Amelia did, but if you cast your mind back to being a child, did you enjoy painting, or cutting and sticking, or simply just baking with a guardian? We spend so much time as adults trying to be 'productive', but that child-like joy of creating something with no consequence is a fantastic way to bring balance to your life.

3. A hobby that keeps you social: when you're feeling exhausted, this can be the trickiest one. It could be as easy as going for a walk with a friend, joining a club, or doing some volunteering. We often spend most of the time that we communicate with others discussing the very topics that cause our stress, so try and create space for those more 'random' conversations.

These types of hobbies can help create a more balanced and fulfilling lifestyle, reducing the risk of burnout. But…by the time you're reading this, it could be too late, and you may be in the clutches of burnout. And we're sorry, we've both been there, and it's consuming. However, you don't have to be there forever, and we want to offer our support, and guidance in getting you on the road back to feeling like 'you'.

In true self-help book style, the first stage is acceptance. Accepting that you're in the depths of burnout is the start of your liberation. You may wish to take some time to write down 'I am burnt out', and a list of the root causes. By being able to visualise the cause of your burnout, you can start to conceptualise it in a way that isn't entirely clouded by your busy mind. This can help you to understand any immediate changes that can be made, but remember, this isn't going to happen overnight-it took you time to become burnt out, and it'll take you time to recover. Now that you have acceptance, a list of the causes, and potential immediate solutions, you can start to evaluate your longer-term options. Do you need to take time off? Do you need to speak to a therapist, or even just a loved one? As we mentioned earlier, it's a team effort, both in the prevention and solution to burn out, and we don't expect you to manage it alone.

The majority of sources that you find online will preach 'self-care' in the recovery of burnout, but what does this actually mean? We could tell you to take a bath, have a cup of tea and do a face mask, but is that going to make an impact-probably not (although we do advocate for cups of tea and baths). One way to practice self-care, is using self-awareness to guide decision making. For example, asking yourself in the morning 'How am I feeling today?' and building your schedule around that, ensuring that you have the necessary breaks and time away from your stressors. Paying close attention to your needs, and acting in a way that prioritises them is a form of self-kindness.

Communication may also be your biggest ally when it comes to conquering burnout. If you need to take time off work, being able to communicate this need is key. Sharing how you're feeling and the challenges you're facing allows others to understand your situation, similar to our section on managing healthcare challenges. Whether it's speaking with a manager, a trusted colleague, or a loved one, expressing your needs helps identify potential adjustments or accommodations that can alleviate stress. For example, discussing workload concerns with your employer could lead to a more manageable distribution of tasks. If you don't feel that you need to bring it to your workplace, talking to friends or family, about your burnout can reduce feelings of isolation and provide emotional relief. Supportive communication fosters a sense of connection, reminding you that you don't have to face burnout alone, and you may find that they've experienced it too, so could offer solutions. But if that's not enough, and you need a professional, there is zero shame in seeking a therapist, or counsellor.

Professionals can provide guidance, science-backed coping mechanisms, and strategies tailored to your situation, helping you manage stress and rebuild your resilience. Having both sought professional support at one point or another, this is their bread and butter, and no concern is ever too small. Our key point around professional help, is that you do not have to stick with the first person you speak to. Much like dating, finding a mental health professional is a two-way street, and requires a mutual 'vibe' (we won't cringe too hard at that) of trust and collaboration, and sometimes, some candid humour.

Ultimately, burnout rehabilitation is a process that calls for perseverance, self-awareness, and sometimes, outside assistance. Overcoming burnout and regaining a sense of balance and fulfilment can be achieved by professional assistance, relying on a support system, or changing your lifestyle. Keep in mind that burnout is a transient state that can be overcome with the correct resources, and that it doesn't define you.

I am struggling to process a significant amount of change in my personal life alongside work, how can I manage this?

Before we start-let's just acknowledge that change is hard. We can all pretend that we absolutely love change, and in small doses it can be revitalising and exciting. But when we are hit with too many changes at once, or even unexpected change, it can be disruptive, scary and even affect your physical and mental wellbeing. 'Change' as a factor can often be forgotten as a viable reason for why people simply aren't themselves, are unhappy, and sometimes even underperforming in the workplace. We want to say that we get it and we are here.

Change can come in lots of shapes and sizes. It can be little, diddy changes, or it can be great, whopper, 'knock you off your feet' style changes. How we have the capacity to handle them depends on how much they actually impact and change our lives, but also our personal resilience and life experiences with change. Examples can include moving house, breaking up with a partner, even having to adapt to a new piece of kit like a laptop or phone. These are all types of change and for some, it is easy to take in your stride. You may get to learn something new, go somewhere different, or learn a new skill. Perhaps you get to project manage and coordinate something you think is just awesome. But for others, even the smallest change can feel unsettling and overstimulating. That is why it's important that when we consider change, and especially when we are coordinating a change, that we appreciate not everyone will be able to embrace it as easily, and so we must plan and offer additional support with that in mind.

Now back to the question itself – managing too many changes. When it is change in both work and personal life, this in itself can be hard, as for many work is a form of grounding, your consistent and known routines and spaces. You know you get up at X time, you go to X place, you work for X amount of time on X pieces and then you go home at X time, where you do XYZ. When this changes, as well as life at home, it is entirely normal to struggle. If you can identify that in yourself and take the time to acknowledge it, that in itself is a huge step. The NHS offers a fabulous resource to support taking stock of how you're feeling. Give their 'Every Mind Matters' website a look and check out their 'Mind Plan'. The plan enables you to share how you're feeling, receive suggestions and advice on what could help you feel better, and then if you opt in, you can receive reminders and mental wellbeing advice to your phone. A fantastic and accessible process to get you started.

It's really important when we are experiencing difficult periods, to find someone you trust and talk to them. It doesn't have to be the instigator of the change; it can be anyone you feel able to express yourself to. You need to let it out. A problem shared is a problem halved. Talk about what worries you, why you feel the way you feel, and if you know, what you need to cope and manage the change. If you don't yet feel able to talk to someone, write it down. Put it out there into the world and own that narrative. The fact is, change wobbles our sense of control, so owning how you feel as a concept in itself, can help you own your next steps. If you did feel slightly bolder, you could talk to the person or even organisation causing the 'change'. Sharing how you feel could open their eyes to the actual impact they're having, could cause them to change their plans, or even make accommodations to lighten the load. You need to get those concerns out there.

The question implied that it's both personal and professional change at hand. Now we have put the 'change' out there through spoken or written word, we need to break it down. Is it that it's too much at once? Is it that it's too big of a change? Or are your feelings a side effect of something else that's going on? We ourselves know, that change can often be a trigger, and it's not the new phone or moving house that's the problem, it's the catalogue of issues that led to it, that have made it the icing on a metaphorical cake. When we dig into this a little deeper, looking after ourselves, identifying looming burnout, saying 'yes' to too many things, can mean when change happens it can all feel like just too much at once. We recommend looking at the 'changes' at hand and trying to identify 'is this the thing that is truly upsetting me or is it more?'. That can often provide a bit of further clarity on what you need to target to get a better grip of the situation.

The most important thing when handling change, is the actual 'coping' part. Now, as we have already said, for some change is just too much and it can affect both physical and mental wellbeing. If this is you, and it is already at the point where your mood, behaviours, and thoughts are changing negatively, please get yourself the help you need. Please speak to a GP, medical professional, or escalate to someone you trust that can get you the support you need. In the front of this book, there are different pathways you can use to talk and get help. Don't do this period of your life alone. If however you are at a point where you are looking to cope and manage yourself through the change, let us share some tips.

Roll it back and focus on the shorter term

When you're feeling overwhelmed, a handful of problems can snowball into what feels like an unmanageable situation. Take a step back and focus on the short term and what you can control within that. What do you need to do today? You can go to bed at a good time, you can shower, you can go to the shops, you can accomplish school pick up. It doesn't have to be huge, but just elements of your life you can control and feel a sense of accomplishment when you've done it. As you roll it back, try to stay in the moment and focus on the here, now, the today. You don't need to think about the past, or the future, just take it day by day.

Acknowledge what you are doing

We love a positivity or gratitude diary and proactive mindfulness. Think, acknowledge, and if possible, write down, every day, what you have accomplished, what you are thankful for. When you're feeling low, sometimes this can be easier said than done, but over time you will curate a beautiful book filled with positive thoughts, accomplishments and future manifestations. Again, the things you callout don't have to be massive, they can be as simple as 'today I cooked a meal for my family'. Mindfulness diaries and the like are relatively inexpensive to buy but a simple notebook can also do the trick. If you take our future advice, you could look at your 'smug' list (in Chapter 4), look at your network, and add the weight of all the amazing things you have accomplished into your positivity list.

Be Flexible

We all have moments of being hard on ourselves. The biggest accommodation we can give to ourselves is just being kind. We don't have all the answers, but we are trying our best. Take regular breaks, ask for help, and build in what we need to get through. This might be asking for reduced hours whilst we resolve whatever is happening, exercising to clear our minds, or even adjusting our working style. With the concept of being flexible on our minds, as part of that we also need to be flexible in our thoughts. Just because we have done one thing one way, doesn't mean we have to always do it that way. Be flexible in the what, why and when, and reframe your mindset to allow for that.

Build out your coping strategies

It's important as you work your way through the stress and upset that comes with change that you acknowledge what helps you to cope. Is it the gym? Is it stepping away from your computer? Is it talking to your partner? Is it an alternative therapy like Reiki? You need to identify these and build them into your routine. Do not let them slip away and always prioritise them. They make you feel stronger and better able to manage, so you need to keep them up.

We hope these help. Again, if it is feeling too much, or your 'struggling' goes on for an extended period, please seek medical advice. You do not have to face this alone, we promise.

I have recently suffered a bereavement, and I'm unsure of how I can process this whilst having to return to 'normal life', any tips?

We read this, and our hearts ache, because we know this feeling all too well. There is nothing that we can say that will remedy the pain that comes with losing a loved one, but we hope that this guidance can serve as a practical aid to start feeling more in control of what is the most out of control life event. On a personal level, we can share that we have been there. Amelia mentioned in her introduction that she lost her grandfather, and that the timing of it was incredibly unfortunate-these things never schedule themselves at a convenient time. Sometimes, 'getting on with things' is the way in which we are able to cope, and so we encourage you to consider what feels right to you, as opposed to seeing anything of what we have written as 'best-practice'…there truly is no 'right' way to grieve.

The first piece of advice that we can give, is to be immensely kind to yourself. This means, giving yourself an allowance to grieve. Giving yourself the time and space to fully experience your feelings is crucial, because grieving is a very personal process. It might be easy to ignore your emotions, particularly if you're under pressure to get back to 'normal life' as soon as possible. There is frequently an unsaid expectation in today's society to move on from loss without dwelling on it. But it's crucial to understand that grieving is a normal, healthy, and human reaction to losing a loved one or something important. It doesn't have a clear schedule or set of guidelines. We encourage you to utilise your company's compassionate leave as much as you need-there is no shame in this! You're going to feel a wide range of complex emotions at different times and to varied intensities-including sadness, despair, rage, guilt, and even relief. All of these are natural feelings. Ignoring or suppressing them may eventually make the healing process more challenging. Give yourself permission to feel these emotions completely. That may look like crying, journaling, or confiding in a trusted person. Every tiny act of expression opens a door for processing your feelings.

In the spirit of being kind to yourself, it's important to be kind as you return to 'normal life', after taking time off. When you are grieving, returning to your daily tasks, be it going back to work, going to school, or taking care of the house, can be difficult and exhausting. It's totally fine if you discover that your motivation, energy, and focus have changed since your loss. During this moment, it's critical to be self-compassionate and try not to pass judgement on yourself. Think about what you could do during the day, such as a walk, or a meditation that takes you out of that routine, and gives you the space to feel any emotions that you might be bottling. Grounding practices can offer a sense of stability and peace when grieving becomes especially strong. Anchoring yourself in the present can be achieved through simple techniques, like repeating mantras, paying attention to your breath, or observing your body's sensations. Take note of your body's feelings, such as the weight of your hands on your lap or the sense of your feet firmly planted on the floor. Another effective way to express yourself is through journaling, which lets you record your feelings, examine your ideas, and track how your grief evolves over time. Documenting your experiences can serve as a helpful reminder that your emotions are real, and a natural part of the healing process. In our experience, by making small, meaningful changes to your day, a mountain of emotions can feel slightly more manageable. Tell people close to you what you need, whether it's more time to finish things, less effort, or just patience and understanding.

Speaking of telling people, grief is one of the most isolating emotions, but that doesn't mean you need to experience it alone. Talking to someone about your feelings and thoughts might provide you much-needed perspective and comfort. Having a network of people who are sympathetic and understand what you're going through is helpful. People who are willing to listen could be close friends, relatives, or even colleagues. It might occasionally be comforting to hear other people's stories and realise that you're not the only one going through difficult circumstances. The emotional load can be lessened just by speaking aloud about the person you've lost or by expressing the feelings you're experiencing. In the context of work, by telling a trusted colleague or manager, you may be given more flexibility, and the space you need to process.

Depending on how you feel, it could be beneficial to get help from a professional grief counsellor or therapist if your grief is too overpowering or is interfering with your day-to-day functioning. The general guidance is that the natural grief process lasts around 6 months, so access to services before then can be limited, but this doesn't mean that it is impossible. If you are struggling prior to this, please contact your GP and they can advise on services in your local area. These experts can lead you through structured discussions, teach techniques for handling strong emotions, and provide you the means to regain stability. There is no right or wrong way to feel grief because it is a complicated and very personal journey. Asking for help only shows how strong you are at identifying when you need more support, not that you're failing. Disrupted sleep, changes in appetite, chronic stress, or persistent exhaustion are some physical manifestations of grief, so take them as your body's warning signs. Asking for assistance is a proactive step towards recovery, and it's perfectly acceptable to get advice from those who can support you during this trying time.

In the longer term, there are going to be moments where you think you're 'over it' (although we never really get over grief, we just learn how to manage it), and then it hits you, like a train. Birthdays, anniversaries, holidays, and other significant occasions can trigger a return of grief, which will most definitely take you by surprise. Even if these situations are difficult, they can be handled through being intentional in your behaviours. Think about how you want to spend these important days in advance. You may want to be around loved ones who support and understand you, or you may want to be by yourself and think in peace. By planning in advance, you can juggle your work alongside the motions of grief.

Chapter 3 - Closing Words

The key takeaway we can keep from this whole chapter is that adversity is really bloody tough. As we said at the very beginning, adversity is a situation you have no choice but to face, even when every fibre of your being wants to run and hide. It can be painful, soul-destroying and limiting, even for the best of us. Many of the Q&As in this section demonstrate exactly that.

We must acknowledge that adversity isn't about quick fix solutions. It takes time, effort, a support network, and personal resilience, to face an adversity head on. It can come in so many shapes and sizes, and can feel different for everyone who experiences it. When we consider this, one key lesson we must never forget, is the sheer importance of taking the time to look after ourselves, our health and our mental wellbeing. It's when these elements fall down, that adversity can be a much bigger hill to climb and even overcome. Additionally, if we know someone is facing their own battles, it's important to be an ally and support where we can.

This chapter is a beacon of hope. You CAN be happy again. You CAN overcome adversity. You CAN find joy in life once more. We hope this chapter not only shared some relatable stories and tips, but that you can see there is light at the end of the tunnel. You don't have to dig deep and accept the cards you've been handed. There are ways out, and more excitingly there is a whole community out there, waiting to support you every step of the way.

4 CAREER GOALS AND EXPECTATION SETTING

Career goals are an interesting topic all in themselves. Often, they are really needed to drive momentum and give you something to focus on, but we also recognise that sometimes, surviving is all you want to accomplish. Sometimes, you are in full swing, smashing your career goals and sometimes they're on hold and you have to pause to focus on other elements of life such as family, health, or personal goals. Sometimes career goals are niche, smaller, and require not as much energy, and sometimes you 'dream big' and have a whopper goal, with lots of interconnected goals that will require a lot of time and effort. What we're trying to get at, is that goals come in lots of shapes and sizes over different expanses of time. But what leads them is your ambition for something more.

It is important to have some kind of 'vision' for your cybersecurity career. If you can, documenting career goals can help to legitimise them and also support your (and your employer's) accountability for working towards them. We have all experienced the joy that is an 'end of year review' or having 'SMART goals'-whilst at the time they can be an absolute pain in the backside, they are actually incredibly important in motivating future you.

Having career goals and associated objectives attached to them provides focus and intentionality to our work life. Whether targeting immediate or future aspirations, each target met propels us towards a broader framework of achievement, and in many cases, an exciting next step down our career pathway. We're going to talk a lot in this section about goal setting, but what are they, and why do we need them?

1. They allow us to evaluate if the opportunities that lay before us are aligned to our aims, or if we're too comfortable, and need to shake things up.
2. Our goals encourage the acquisition of abilities and skillsets. For example, if the goal is to reach a specific role, but you need to have XYZ qualification

to have it, then you can plan for that.

3. Importantly, goals allow us to give ourselves a much needed 'pat on the back'. There is nothing quite like ticking an achievement off the list and allowing ourselves to feel good about an accomplishment.
4. Goals allow us to create life and career priorities. What needs to come first, what can wait, what will make us happy?

Most importantly, goals stimulate self-progress. Objectives give us the chance to seek new experiences for learning, encourage us to network and foster new relationships, to find new sources and information to help us accomplish what we need. They enable us to become better cybersecurity professionals and better empowered individuals.

On to some questions...

I feel stuck in my current role, but don't know how to take control of my career path. How can I start making decisions that align with my long-term goals in cybersecurity?

We're genuinely pleased to have the opportunity to delve into this topic because it's something we've both personally experienced. It's an area that can feel especially tricky to navigate, particularly if you're earlier on in your career journey. Neither of us started out with a clearly defined 'dream role' in cybersecurity. Instead, our careers have grown organically over time. However, we understand the feeling of being 'stuck' in a role that you know is merely a stepping stone toward your dream job. This is a common challenge faced by professionals, not just within cybersecurity but across many industries.

To take control of your career path, the first step is gaining clarity on where you'd ultimately like to end up. This doesn't have to be as specific as identifying a particular job title or organisation. Instead, you can start by asking yourself, 'what excites me about cybersecurity?' You might discover that you absolutely love diving deep into the technical aspects, or perhaps you're captivated by the art of communicating security strategies to the business side of an organisation. Whatever it is that sparks your enthusiasm when you think or talk about it, that's likely your 'thing.'

It's also perfectly normal if, at this stage, you're not entirely sure what excites you enough to build a career around. If that's the case, allow yourself the space and time to explore and reflect. Identifying what you truly enjoy is a critical foundational step that will enable you to make informed decisions about your future path.

Next, let's discuss an insightful piece of advice shared by a former manager: consider where you want to be long-term, not just professionally, but personally as well. While it can sometimes feel frustrating to be asked about personal plans, like family goals, during career discussions, the intention behind our advice is constructive. For example, let's say one of your personal goals is to buy a house within the next 3 years. To achieve this, you might determine that you need a job paying £50,000 annually. In this scenario, you could target roles that align with this salary requirement to meet your goal. The key takeaway is that your personal aspirations can and should guide your career decisions, ensuring your work aligns with and supports your broader life objectives.

Once you've reflected on what excites you and considered the practical aspects tied to your personal goals, it's time to evaluate where you currently stand. For instance, imagine one of us realised we needed a long-term contract to support buying a home and had a passion for data protection. The question then becomes: 'what steps would we need to take to align our career with both our passion and our personal goal?'

This is where conducting a thorough skills and experience review becomes invaluable. Consider asking yourself the following questions:

1. What skills or certifications are necessary for the roles I aspire to, and how does my current skillset compare to the requirements listed in job descriptions for those positions?
2. Are there specific projects, responsibilities, or achievements in my current role that align with my future goals? How can I leverage these opportunities to build relevant experience?

During this process, you'll likely identify gaps in your skill set, certifications, or experience required for your desired roles. This is completely normal and part of the journey. Identifying these gaps empowers you to take control by actively working to fill them.

Start by setting incremental goals, perhaps in 90-day intervals, that map out actionable steps to address these gaps. For example, you might pursue certifications, engage in online learning, network with industry peers, or even take on pro-bono projects to build experience. This is also an excellent point to consider seeking a mentor. A mentor can provide valuable guidance, help you set realistic goals, and hold you accountable as you work toward them.

We'd like to address the feeling of being 'stuck.' This often stems from a sense of stagnation or lack of progress. By creating a plan and proactively engaging in your own development, you give yourself a sense of purpose and forward momentum. Staying busy with meaningful tasks that contribute to your growth can help alleviate boredom or feeling stuck.

You've done all of this great work, but what happens now? Establish quarterly check-ins to guide your development, whether that involves sitting down with a trusted colleague or friend and discussing them, or taking time for yourself. Regularly review and reflect on your career goals to ensure they remain aligned with both your evolving interests (both in the workplace and at home), and the ever-changing trends within the industry. This approach not only keeps your growth on track, but ensures your efforts are strategically focused on achieving your long-term aspirations.

And finally, it's important to recognise that your long-term career goals are not set in stone and can evolve as you gain new experiences. As we said earlier, shifting your perspective, and subsequently, your career goal is entirely normal and in lots of ways expected. Trust yourself!

There are so many certifications and 'skillsets' in cybersecurity. How do I figure out which ones actually matter for progressing in my career?

This is tricky. Let us explain why.

For some roles, a cybersecurity qualification is necessary. An example could be if you were working in Cyber Forensics, having a certification and security clearances that show you can appropriately handle, view, and manage forensic evidence could be a requirement. This also applies to gaining accreditations or being professionally registered, for example, you may wish to gain a professional registration title such as Chartered, Principal or Associate via the UK Cyber Security Council, a requirement for certain roles and organisations. Note though, that this is in specific cybersecurity specialisms, and so having that under your belt could help you progress in your field, but it isn't essential for everyone.

What makes it tricky, is that we have noticed professionals of all genders grabbing and, in some cases, hoarding up certifications, not because they need them, but because it makes them feel comfortable to be in industry. And this matter disproportionately impacts women. It ties to self-doubt, the urge to justify why they need a seat at the table, the comfort in feeling like you deserve to be part of the cybersecurity conversation. If this is the reason why you're considering certifications, then please think again. You are more than qualified, and you more than deserve to have a voice in the cybersecurity space. For these kinds of feelings, it again may be better to speak with your manager or mentor, to address how to get you out of this headspace and instead feeling comfortable and able to progress as you are.

There is much to be said for on-the-job learning. We have both benefitted from learning as we go from those around us. Whilst we all can grab a textbook and study consistently, there is nothing better than a lived experience. Finding a good buddy in your organisation and having a 'ride along' where you can shadow what they're doing, or having them train you on tools and technologies, can offer you just as much if not more than a cybersecurity qualification.

When mentees talk to us about certifications, we recommend really understanding the cybersecurity position you're aiming for, and doing your research into recommended certifications and skills. This can be done by asking others working in the role what they have and if it's helped, mooching through LinkedIn at those in the 'dream role' and seeing what that have, or looking at resources such as those provided through a professional body. Create a list of the qualifications and certifications you're seeing and take a deeper dive into what they offer, if they are 'recognised' in industry as a valuable certification, and also if financially they are attainable.

We recognise that for some, self-funding a certification simply isn't possible. With that in mind, we want to highlight that you don't have to spend a fortune on cybersecurity qualifications to add a depth or skill to your portfolio. If you're working towards a degree because that's a goal, then great, but organisations like FutureLearn, Cybrary, Microsoft and MITRE offer so many free courses which are excellent additions to your CV. Additionally, whilst some certification vendors like you to do both the learning and exam with them, there are many that can be used solely as an exam provider. As an example, if we think about CISSP, there are lots of free resource, YouTube videos, mentors and books out there which you can use to study, and then pay for the exam itself to gain the qualification. This is something to consider if you're thinking of taking that pathway. Please don't spend a fortune on qualifications until you know they're actually what you need, and only if they won't put you into financial hardship.

We've delved into getting certifications, and we have both benefited from them, but we do believe that cybersecurity careers and progression are more than having a list of certifications. With neither of us coming from traditional cybersecurity backgrounds (the analyst way up), we have done very well through mentoring, shadowing, tailored studying, and on-the-job learning. This is what makes it tricky. It's hard to advocate for certain courses, when we're not entirely sure we believe in them ourselves! We therefore won't use this space to callout any specific qualifications and instead leave you to think about what we have said and make a decision.

To end with skillsets, if we are talking coding, being able to write Python or understanding cloud environments, they might be important skills to gain. If these are needed in order for you to progress, and you've done your research to validate this…go for it! However, what often goes unnoticed, but is actually critical to successful careers in cybersecurity, are your core skills (some refer to them as soft skills but think that makes them sound fluffy!) Core skills are traits, behaviours and attributes which allow a professional to interact and work effectively with those around them as people. Great examples of this include being emotionally intelligent, being able to communicate to different audiences, or to be an effective organiser. For many, these may seem like a perk, rather than an essential, but if we reflect on the idea of a cybersecurity breach, having an individual in the room who may not have a CISSP, but instead can rally individuals, effectively communicate to customers, and show empathy to victims may carry more weight.

Building core skills comes from lived experiences, being in tune with your personality and brand, and through self-development techniques. We've both benefitted from techniques such as manifestation, practising the art of active listening, and having a clear set of methodologies to organise and maintain momentum in our projects. Being well rounded and having your core skills flexed can be more powerful than a bunch of qualifications or certifications. Think about what would help you to succeed and also what would help you to distinguish yourself when navigating your career.

My end-of-year review is coming up, and I want to ask for a promotion and a raise. How can I build a compelling case that highlights my value to the company?

We love to see women take control of their reviews, and we're not seeing it enough!

To effectively broach the topic of a promotion and/or a raise, it's crucial to present a well-prepared, compelling case that clearly demonstrates your value to the company whilst aligning your contributions with its goals-sounds super easy, right? Whilst it may sound easy to get 1,2 and 3 done to get to 4, it's realistically completely out of our nature as human beings to self-promote!

This is where, the term, 'smug' list may be your saviour. A term coined by Amelia's Mum, your smug list is the process of documenting your achievements over the past year, as and when they happen. Make a list, create a file, pop it in an excel spreadsheet. A smug list could include quite literally anything that you have done that has been positive, and don't stop at your workload-perhaps you've been a pillar of the team for new joiners, or provided mentoring to others…if you've done it, it's going on the list.

Next is to match those 'smugs' to measurable impacts-things that show what you've done made an actual difference. Callouts can include meeting or exceeding targets, solving critical challenges, or contributing to continual improvements. Grab the evidence that proves the smug in question, be it numerical, or a screenshot of a nice piece of feedback via message or email and put them together as examples that can be used to show how you shine!

Finally, match your 'smugs' to the objectives of the business. Examine the organisation's goals and strategic priorities. Then, relate your accomplishments to those. With any organisation, your argument for promotion or more money, is strengthened if you can show how your job directly contributes to the company's success. For example, if improving security metrics is a top priority for the organisation, highlight how your work has contributed to this. By demonstrating this link, you establish yourself as a strategic asset to the business rather than just an employee.

This process can be a great way to see where you're making an impact, but also where you are lacking achievements to use in your case. Here's where you harness the art of continual improvement, and you set some short-term goals. You may wish to use a framework like SMART (Specific, Measurable, Attainable, Relevant, Time-bound) to articulate these goals. For example, you might say, 'by the end of 2025, I want to lead a cybersecurity team that develops proactive defence strategies to reduce incidents by 30%.' You can then drill into the shorter-term objectives that feed into you making this goal. By articulating these goals and objectives to your manager, you highlight that you have a roadmap for your future and that you are committed to growing. You show that you've really thought about what you want to be and how you plan to get there. You don't have to have met these goals to be promoted, but demonstrating commitment, and a plan, will work in your favour when it comes to that promotion chat.

As you're approaching the scheduled conversation, we'd advise you to make a two-pronged business case. On one hand, describe how your promotion helps the business, for example, by giving you the opportunity to manage high-impact projects which can improve team productivity. With the other hand, have supporting points you've gathered from your smug list that demonstrate how you've either successfully done it before, or your plan to get the relevant experience through your objectives.

When preparing to discuss a salary increase, use resources like Glassdoor to benchmark your pay to industry norms for your position and area in order to give you a tangible idea of what you should be asking for, backed up by real-world statistics. The return on your organisation's investment in you is the main focus of this strategy when discussing both topics.

Getting feedback from dependable mentors or coworkers can also help you make a stronger argument. Give them access to your draft promotion document to get their feedback or to find out about other accomplishments that you might have missed is a fantastic way to get a 'fresh pair of eyes' on your approach. Also, if you are comfortable, asking if they would ask as a reference, advocate, or depending on role in the organisation, a sponsor, could be a gamechanger for your promo or pay rise request.

Lastly, practice your proposal to make sure it is clear and assured. Highlight your importance to the business and how your development fits in with its objectives. To have the most impression, schedule your conversation for a suitable time, such as after finishing a significant project or during your yearly review. Write a written summary of the meeting after the discussion, restating your goals, accomplishments, and the next steps that were addressed.

So, you've done all of that, but your management isn't completely onboard. How do you handle this? Preparing in advance with a few intelligent answers for any possible criticisms can help you to go into the situation with more confidence. For instance, highlight your efforts that have reduced expenses or increased revenue if your manager expresses worries about budgetary concerns. This proactive planning ahead will show that you have considered the viewpoint of the business and are prepared to respond to problems in a constructive manner.

If, despite your preparation and efforts, your request for a promotion or raise is met with a definitive 'no', it's time to take a step back and evaluate your next move. In order to completely comprehend the decision, start by asking for helpful criticism. Ask specifically about your areas of improvement, whether there is a timeframe for reviewing your request, and whether there are any specific goals you 'must meet' in order to be given consideration for promotion. Even if you're disappointed, this demonstrates professionalism and growth readiness.

As hard as it is, it could be time to determine whether your organisation supports your long-term professional objectives. Think about your priorities: do you think there are chances for growth in other sectors of the company? Does the leadership and culture of the organisation encourage your professional growth? If not, start looking into outside possibilities where your efforts and abilities would be better appreciated. Keep in mind that continuing to work in a position where your efforts are routinely disregarded will impede your ability to advance in your career and find fulfilment in your work. Long-term success depends on finding the ideal setting to develop your abilities!

Ultimately, the more proactivity you show, the more likely you are to achieve either a promotion or a raise, and we believe that by being objective about your achievements and value is a key method of winning what you're looking for. We can't dress up that having conversations around your careers, and even more so, money, can be uncomfortable-imagine though, that by putting your head above the parapet and by advocating for yourself that something truly exciting happens. The chat may be uncomfortable, but the outcome potentially lifechanging. Go into the chat with a positive hat on, share the vision with supported goals, planning and smugs, and whatever the outcome, assess if you're satisfied and if you're needs have been met. Be brave, be bold, be accountable.

I've been offered a great cybersecurity role, but it clashes with my personal values and priorities. How do I decide what's truly non-negotiable and when to compromise?

You have a brilliant role land on your lap, but it conflicts with who you are or need to be. This is more common than you can imagine. A fantastic example are roles which require lots of travel. For many of us, a job uptown would be incredible, but actually we need the flexibility to be at home to look after our loved ones, which an onsite role couldn't support. So, what do you do?

The first piece of advice we can give is to document your non-negotiables. These are elements of your life that need to be satisfied to make you happy and able to function. Non-negotiables cannot be negotiated. They matter to you so much that when asked to compromise, your gut tells you 'no'. A few examples of these from our own lives:

- My working hours have to be X because of the school run.
- I want to be office based as I find I work better and it taps into my social needs.
- I must earn X amount of money so I can have X lifestyle.
- The role must be in X region otherwise I can't make it work.

After non-negotiables, you can consider the 'needs' you have for a role. These are elements of a job, such as tasks or structures that you would look for in your 'ideal' role. These again, are important to identify as they help you look at different jobs and understand if the role is authentically you. For example:

- I like to be client facing and so I want to spend my time collaborating with victims.
- I like to use XYZ tools and so I want to have that as part of my role.
- I struggle with numbers so I don't want a role where I have to manage budget or finance.

Intrinsically tied to our non-negotiables and role needs, are our personal values and priorities. They guide what cannot be negotiated, what we want to do with our time in the day to day, and ultimately where the line in the sand is for what is right or wrong for us. These are at our core, and part of our personality. They make us who we are. They can be tied to our family settings, our religions or belief systems, to our gender roles, and even our connections to the community around us. Whilst this all sounds very profound, our values and priorities shift. They can evolve, develop, and alter with different life experiences and changes in our circumstances.

Now, going back to the question. A role is available but it clashes with personal values and priorities. How do I decide what's non-negotiable and what to flex on?

When you look at the position, what values and priorities does it go against? Are these intrinsic to who you are? If you went against these values and priorities, would the sacrifice be a non-negotiable, and would that be too much to bear? If we look at the previous non-negotiable example of dropping children to school, yes it must happen, yes you must do that before you go to work, but could you use a different mechanism to make that happen? Could a friend help or a breakfast club? Would your children suffer from you not doing the run? Could you do some of them and others someone else help you with, so therefore you could negotiate with a potential employer? Are your children a year away from secondary school where they won't need dropping anymore?

Look at your non-negotiables and see where you could bend versus where the hard line lies. This should help you in getting the clarity you need to decide if you should take the position or be flexible to the request.

We can't tell you where to compromise. All we can say is, don't compromise if you think you will regret it. If something matters to you that much, a job role should not come above it. You need to satisfy all elements of who you are for you to be successful. Take your time, write it down, talk it through with someone you trust. Additionally, don't feel guilty about being transparent with anyone waiting on your decision relating to a role application or even rejecting a role opportunity. If a company truly values you, they may be willing to accommodate your non-negotiables, so don't be afraid to ask. You must be certain.

After taking a year off to focus on personal growth, I'm worried about how to explain this career gap on my CV when applying for cybersecurity jobs. What's the best approach?

First, let us say that taking a year out for personal growth is nothing to feel ashamed or defensive about. In fact, career breaks are increasingly common nowadays, and often seen as a sign of self-awareness and commitment to longer term goals. Your time away can actually be an asset to you, as long as you frame it correctly. There isn't a particularly long answer to this, but we can offer some pointers!

When addressing the gap on your CV, try to be honest but strategic. A concise explanation such as 'I took time off to focus on personal development, including skill-building and certifications relevant to cybersecurity' can turn a potential red flag into a talking point that highlights your initiative and drive to longer-term success. If you engaged in any activities that align with your professional growth, like completing courses, earning certifications, contributing to open-source projects, or even volunteering in tech-related roles, make sure to spotlight those. Employers will value the skills and self-motivation you demonstrated during that time.

It's also essential to focus on what you bring to the table as a result of this time off. Tailor your CV to showcase your recent skills, certifications, and accomplishments. For instance, by emphasising relevant technical expertise or any hands-on experience that directly aligns with the roles you're targeting, demonstrates how that time was valuable to your development. Highlighting the ways you've stayed engaged with the field can help shift attention from the gap, to your benefits.

When the topic comes up in interviews, and it will, be confident and prepared. Frame your time off as a deliberate choice to align your personal and professional goals, emphasising the clarity and renewed energy it gave you. Share specific examples of how this period helped you grow, whether through enhancing core skills like problem-solving or pursuing technical advancements. Employers value candidates who are reflective, adaptable, and forward-thinking, all traits that such a break can showcase.

It is important to recognise that 'time out' isn't necessarily due to personal development or bettering ourselves. Often, people step away from organisations due to significant life changes such as bereavements or caregiving responsibilities. As an example, we know many individuals who have stepped out of cybersecurity to raise a family.

What we have listed above can be challenging to apply and practice, particularly with parental leave. You can feel like your career has been on hold. Stepping out to have babies is wonderful, but really can be an identity crisis all in itself! Please do not doubt that you have picked up new skills and attributes from that chapter in your life. You may not have been studying for a cybersecurity qualification, but you have been growing small people! It's not an easy job and you most definitely haven't been relaxing with their feet up. In an interview, own the reason you have been away. Own that you have gone through a new experience in your life, and, if comfortable, share that experience and what you learnt with the person asking. If that recruiter or employer is 'off' or 'unhappy' with your reason for being out, ESPECIALLY if a career gap is to do with caregiving or having babies, then you probably didn't want to work there anyway!

Ultimately, the ideal approach is to be authentic, whilst demonstrating that you're ready to contribute intentionally to your next role. Your time off doesn't define your career, see it as just one chapter of your larger story.

Chapter 4 - Closing Words

We wanted to stress that when you are thinking of career goals and expectation setting, they need to be authentic to you. It is all well and good your Mum telling you she wants you to be a Brain Surgeon, but does this actually fit with what you want? Would it bring you joy? It would be lovely to know that your manager believes you'd be a fabulous SOC analyst, but deep down, if this is of no interest to you, why would you consent to it being a documented career goal?

Your career goals need to inspire YOU to make them happen.

- 100% dream big.
- 100% be hopeful.
- 100% be courageous.
- 100% don't be held back but others visions and idealisms for you.

100% hone in on what excites you about cybersecurity and dig into that.

And most importantly, tell others about the ambition! Make sure that your leader knows your goals and objectives, and champions you within the workplace. Make sure your support network knows so they can advocate and elevate you. They say it takes a village, right?

To end this chapter, we wanted to provide some example career objectives you can strive for. Unless you are a pro when it comes to setting goals, it can be quite tasking. Some examples of goals that we have used in the past include:

- Enhancing our leadership skills. Excitingly, this ties to where we first met at Empowering You. In our strives to be more empowered leaders, we joined a course and found a whole new network of superstars along the way.
- To deliver a TEDx talk. This was one of Rebecca's career goals and she's only gone and done it! Check the link to her talk in the references section!
- To be a cybersecurity focussed entrepreneur or non-profit founder...why hello Amelia!
- To gain new technical qualifications to support cybersecurity knowledge and understanding, whether it be SANS, Cybrary or LinkedIn Learning.
- To work on our public speaking. We have had professional coaches and mentors in this space and have attended skills workshops. This is a fantastic one if you're wanting to build out your professional cybersecurity brand and image.

These career goals inspired us, which is why they have worked. Maybe they'll inspire you? If not, take some time to sit down and identify what the vision is… and then get documenting!

One final point, as we mentioned above, your interests and priorities may shift, and that's perfectly natural. You shouldn't feel pressured to stick to a path that no longer excites or fulfils you. Embracing flexibility allows you to adapt your goals to reflect what truly matters to you at any given stage in life. Changing your mind isn't a setback, it's a sign of growth and self-awareness, enabling you to pursue a career that aligns with who you are and what you value most.

5 SHINING A LIGHT - CYBER ROLE MODELS

We have taken you on a very real journey in this book and imparted our fair share of wisdom and lived experiences. We have also said, more than once, that you are not alone. We are certain that many of the stories and examples we have shared have resonated because you too have experienced them firsthand, be it the good, the bad…or the ugly!

We have been able to dig through and find the hope and motivation to forge our own careers, as well as making our contributions to protecting others through our work, because of the inspiring individuals and role models who have wrapped their arms around us-the ones who have made sure that we ourselves were not alone. The cybersecurity industry is vast and there is a huge group of people ready to help you fight the good fight and be the person you strive to be.

With that in mind, we wanted to use this section as a spotlight. We want to introduce you to individuals we believe to be aspirational and inspirational. Individuals who are role models, making waves in cybersecurity. Some are established in cybersecurity, and some are making new footprints. Each person in this section, however, is a gamechanger, a beacon and an advocate. We encourage you to look them up, follow them, and, if you're feeling brave to send them a message.

We are proud to know each of them, and hope in them sharing their experiences, that you can see more than ever, that you are not alone in your career.

Disclaimer-The responses in this section to the questions, are the respondent's own perspectives and opinions.

Laura Reilly

We see you as a role model because of all the amazing work you do in the cybersecurity industry! Tell the readers a little about you and your cybersecurity career to date.

Hi, I'm Laura! I'm currently working as the Head of Marketing at Cyro Cyber, a managed security services provider. But my career in the cybersecurity industry was quite honestly an accident! As a humanities focussed student (one who didn't enjoy IT/sciencey subjects), cybersecurity was never a consideration of where I might end up. I had many ideas over the years: an author, actress, teacher, journalist, and eventually, marketing-but even then, I was hoping to market within the film/TV/literature space!

I studied English Literature and Creative Writing at the University of Surrey and undertook a Professional Training Year, where I decided I wanted to pursue a marketing career. As such, I began searching for marketing roles, when all of a sudden, COVID hit, hiring freezes happened, and I was an English student with no experience… it felt like I was never going to find a job!

Finally, after 10 months of continually applying and over 50 rejections, I secured my first role as a Digital Marketing Associate at a cybersecurity recruitment agency. I'll be honest-although I was so grateful to have a job, I was at first, a little disheartened that the inception of my career wasn't what I expected. Cyber wasn't part of my plan. What did I know about it? How would

I ever do this job? Despite my intense imposter syndrome, I decided to give it a go.

In my first role, I was brought in to set up the marketing function. I had no prior marketing experience. I had only a hunger to learn and lots of energy and ideas. This served me well. Within three years, I had built a marketing function, and bought in three new team members to help me deliver on my strategy. Some of the elements of this strategy included: establishing a strong online presence (building LinkedIn followers from 3,000 to 43,000 organically); creating valuable content (videos, carousel posts, eBooks, blogs) for job seekers; establishing and leading industry partnerships with prominent cybersecurity organisations, including CAPSLOCK, Ada Scotland, Women in Cyber Security (WiCyS UK&I), and ISC2; delivering numerous talks on personal branding to UK university students and CAPSLOCK cohorts; and building the InClusive inCyber (ICIC) community from the ground up, a community of 400+ women in cybersecurity.

Every quarter, I hosted networking breakfasts in London and Manchester, providing a safe, supportive space for women to share their stories, successes, and challenges, and for them to meet allies and lifelong friends. The events were designed to bolster attendee's confidence, helping them realise that there's no limit to what they can achieve in cybersecurity and lessen the talent gap.

In March 2024, I was brought into Cyro Cyber to build their marketing function, again from scratch. Honestly, at the start, I felt HUGE imposter syndrome. I didn't feel I knew enough about cybersecurity to be effective in the job and I didn't want to let Cyro down. Luckily, I had the best friends, allies and mentors around me, Cyro included, who were incredibly supportive and bolstered me every step of the way. So I took the job, and within a year, through a combination of strategic planning and a commitment to meaningful industry relationships, I've achieved more than I ever thought I could, such as doubling our LinkedIn following, leading three community events, and establishing the Cyro Chapter-a community that fosters thought leadership across the cybersecurity security landscape. I've also led mine, and Cyro's, first ever appearance at a trade show, the International Cyber Expo 2024. This was probably the most challenging project I've worked on to date, but seeing the stand on the day made it all so worth it.

And this is where I am now, still plugging away! Even now, I still face that imposter syndrome daily, but I've learned that it's not about knowing everything-it's about having the right people around you and trusting in your journey. With the right mindset and support, the sky truly is the limit.

Life is not always straightforward. Share a challenge you have faced which has impacted your career, and if you can, what you did to get past it.

Like many women in the industry, I've struggled with imposter syndrome all my life. I constantly feel like I don't deserve the praise and success I've had and I'm very much waiting for the day that I'm exposed as a fraud!

There was a specific point in time that my work on the InClusive InCyber events started picking up traction, and the praise and positive feedback suddenly picked up too. It was 100% the best scenario I could've asked for, but it was also overwhelming, because I found it very difficult to see the truth in what people were saying. 'They're just being polite' or 'they don't really understand what I do', were two reasons I often used (and still do!) to explain praise away, which is so detrimental for self-confidence, assurance and decision making.

Since this time, the recognition I've received has only grown. Whether through winning awards, being invited to speak at industry events, or even taking on new roles and jobs, I've had extensive proof from multiple people in this industry truly believing in me. While there will never be adequate words to express my gratitude, or to express how much it helps my confidence, it also brings great pressure. The last thing I want to do is let anyone down, and I've learned quite quickly that the perception I have of myself doesn't match that of others. From speaking to other women in cybersecurity, I know that I'm not alone in this and it's a real problem that can genuinely be debilitating.

So, how do I mitigate this? By leaning on trusted mentors, friends, and allies in the industry, who are able to see an objective view of my skills and capabilities. People I've worked with, alongside, or in collaboration with-people qualified to make a judgement (them being 'qualified' is important, in order for you to trust it.) If the feedback is all consistent (which it usually is), why should I not believe it? They believe in me, so I should believe in me too. It's really okay to ask for help, we all need it sometimes, and it's what friends are for.

I recently came across an approach that truly spoke to me. Instead of disbelieving positive feedback straight away, tell yourself: 'this is their perspective. Maybe they see something in me that I haven't fully accepted yet.' I love this because, when we dismiss the praise or feedback from those we trust, we're not only doing ourselves a disservice, but them as well. By doubting their words, we're essentially questioning their judgment and sincerity. These are the people who are investing time, energy, and care into supporting us, and by dismissing their insights, we undermine their perspective and trust. Why would we assume they're lying to us? When we reject their positive feedback, we not only limit our own growth, but fail to honour the value they're trying to offer -

and you'd never do that intentionally. I always try to give myself this reality check when I feel the doubt creeping in. It certainly helps!

The other thing I do that works wonders is to document everything-the praise people give you, positive feedback from managers, key metrics you've produced, tangible impacts on a project, or someone's career, etc. Store them in a journal, or a folder on your laptop and have them ready for the days that you're lacking confidence, ready to refer back to. Sometimes, all you need is a reminder!

We think you shine! Share a moment in your career where you felt you turned a corner and you have achieved something you're proud of.

My goodness, can I have a few? My career has only been 4.5 years long so far, but there are a few moments that really make all of the hard work so worth it.

The first would be building InClusive InCyber. It has arguably become one of the fastest-growing, women-centric initiatives in the cybersecurity security sector. What began as a spark of inspiration in my bedroom, through the desire to create a more inclusive, peer-driven community for women in cybersecurity, has evolved into something much greater than I could have EVER imagined.

I've always been passionate about fostering an *actual* community. Networking events are great, but sometimes, they can feel impersonal. I was dedicated to making sure that wasn't the case with ICIC. The events are inclusive spaces to hear other women's journeys, and get inspired. Curating these impactful experiences and witnessing the genuine professional relationships that have emerged has been deeply fulfilling. ICIC has grown beyond a mere networking platform; it's become a movement for advocacy, empowerment, and opportunity. Having developed it from an idea to the beautiful group it is today is not only a highlight of my career, but of my life.

Another proud milestone came in April 2024, when I was invited to take on the role of Marketing Lead for WiCyS UK+I. In less than a year, I've developed a comprehensive marketing plan that aims to build brand awareness. Some of these new initiatives include my WiCyS Wisdom blog series, which amplifies insights from senior women leaders in cybersecurity, a variety of webinars, community meetups, and consistent LinkedIn content. Through this strategy and the team's combined efforts, we've seen membership grow from 322 to 858 in 12 months!

Additionally, being invited to be a panellist for Eleanor Dallaway's 'Grab the Mic' panel at the International Cyber Expo 2024, to share insights on balancing career and life from an often forgotten (or misunderstood) Gen Z perspective, was undoubtedly a fangirl moment. I've loved Eleanor's podcast for a while, so it was an honour to share my experiences, particularly to represent the younger portion of the workforce. I feel that these important conversations don't always take younger perspectives into consideration, or they just get forgotten. But we are the future of the workforce, and our opinions are strong, innovative and worth hearing.

Finally, winning Cyber Marketeer of the Year at the 'Most Inspiring Women in Cyber Awards' in February 2024 was probably the most surreal and emotional moment of my career so far. When my name was announced, I was completely stunned - 'there's no way', I thought. I've always felt that my life's purpose has been to help people, and hearing how women have found friends, mentors, and even new jobs through the community I built is all the recognition I could ever hope for. Knowing that the women in cybersecurity initiatives that I've been part of have made a real difference in people's lives is what drives me every day. I never expected to be awarded for something I loved so much, so receiving this honour meant more than I could ever express.

I feel incredibly grateful to be part of so many incredible initiatives. Each holds a special place in my heart because they represent my passion for fostering diversity, creating meaningful opportunities, and driving positive change in this industry. The connections I've built, the stories I've heard and above all, the friends I've made, is why I love being part of this industry with every beat of my heart.

When you're old and grey, and you look back over what we are sure will be an epic cybersecurity career, what would you like your legacy to look like? Is there anything in particular you'd like to have accomplished?

It's weird to even think that I might have a legacy, but it's a truly lovely thought. I hope people remember me for doing good-for actually making a positive impact on others' lives. To me, kindness isn't a finite resource, and I've always believed that it should be given freely and often, especially in a world where things can be so tough sometimes. I want to be remembered as someone who genuinely cared about people-someone who was always ready to give a compliment, lend support, or make an introduction, because I truly believe we all do better when we help each other.

I'd love to be remembered as a pillar of the community. While I hope that over my career, I will truly hone my marketing capabilities and continue to improve my craft (and hopefully be remembered for this too!), for me, it's more than that. I want to be someone who wasn't just about work or glitzy awards or titles, rather, someone who helped people feel valued, connected, and empowered. I want to be the person who brought people together, helped them grow, and made their lives and careers better in meaningful ways. If I could be that person who encouraged someone to keep going when they felt like giving up, or who helped them see their own potential when they couldn't, that would mean everything to me.

Above all, I want to inspire women of all ages, backgrounds, and experiences to know that they can do anything they set their mind to, as long as they have the right mindset and the support system to back them up. I want to show them that they're never alone, and that having doubts or that voice of imposter syndrome doesn't mean they're not capable and it doesn't mean they can't succeed.

I've been so fortunate to have had so many incredible women in this industry believe in me, give me their time, share their expertise, and support me in ways that I'll never be able to repay. Therefore, if I can do that for even just one other person, I'll retire happy, knowing I gave back to this industry in the same way that others have given to me.

That's what I hope my legacy will be-kindness, connection, and empowering others to be the best version of themselves.

Radhika Modha

We see you as a role model because of all the amazing work you do in the cybersecurity industry! Tell the readers a little about you and your cybersecurity career to date.

I didn't start my career in cybersecurity-I began in finance. Early on, I completed an ACA training contract and qualified as a chartered accountant, working in risk assurance at a 'Big Four' firm before transitioning into internal audit in industry. During this time, I focused heavily on risk management, controls, and leveraging data analytics to identify trends. This analytical approach led me to investigate systems more deeply, tracing root causes and uncovering vulnerabilities. The more I explored, the more fascinated I became with how systems and networks could be accessed-or even manipulated for various purposes. Working across companies of different sizes, I frequently encountered unique and unexpected issues with far-reaching impacts. Sharing these insights with colleagues only deepened my interest, ultimately leading me to transition into cybersecurity.

In my current role as a Group Business Information Security Officer (BISO), I bridge the gap between security considerations and business strategy, drawing on my deep commercial and process knowledge to align security initiatives with broader business objectives. I also work closely with our group businesses to strengthen governance, risk, and compliance, ensuring security is embedded across all facets of the organisation.

Life is not always straightforward. Share a challenge you have faced which has impacted your career, and if you can, what you did to get past it.

One of the biggest challenges I faced when transitioning into cybersecurity was feeling like everyone was speaking a different language. Conversations about seemingly simple concepts would quickly dive into deep technical detail and jargon, making me question whether I had made the right decision. I wasn't sure if I would ever think or communicate in the same way as my more technical colleagues.

Rather than letting this hold me back, I leaned into my strengths, particularly my ability to quickly understand and assess complex topics from my experience in audit. I embraced simplicity, actively listening to the technical discussions to learn, but always bringing conversations back to fundamental principles when it came to decision-making. By relating technical details to business risk and broader operational impact, I not only improved my own understanding but also helped technical teams step back from the weeds and see the bigger picture.

Over time, this approach shifted the focus of our discussions from pure technical configurations to real business outcomes, preventing conversations from becoming overly circular or lost in the details. It also helped me build strong relationships, as the person who could bridge the gap between risk, business operations, and security strategy-something that has now become one of my greatest strengths.

We think you shine! Share a moment in your career where you felt you turned a corner and you have achieved something you're proud of.

A key turning point for me was being invited to speak at security events and participate in industry panels based on my experience. Coming from a finance and audit background, I initially struggled with imposter syndrome, feeling that I didn't have the same technical depth as others in the field. At the time, I hadn't fully appreciated how varied perspectives are just as valuable as technical expertise in cybersecurity.

Public speaking has never come naturally to me. I still experience a form of stage fright when addressing large groups-but I've learnt to work through it. I'm incredibly grateful to the security community and my employer for their support and encouragement along the way.

As I gained experience, I realised that my ability to translate complex security concepts into business risks and opportunities was a critical strength. I also discovered that many others in the industry shared the same imposter syndrome I did. Instead of letting it hold me back, I used it as motivation to lean into discomfort, develop my communication skills, and actively engage with the community by attending and speaking at events.

This growth has had a direct impact on my day-to-day work. I'm more confident engaging with senior leadership, framing cybersecurity discussions around financial impact, operational resilience, and strategic priorities. Over time, I've spoken on industry panels, led internal security awareness initiatives, and helped shape security strategy at an organisational level.

When you're old and grey, and you look back over what we are sure will be an epic cybersecurity career, what would you like your legacy to look like? Is there anything in particular you'd like to have accomplished?

I want to look back and know that I played a part in helping people and businesses build with confidence, without the fear that a cybersecurity incident could undo everything they've worked for. I want to shift the perception of security-when done right, it should enable innovation, not just be a tick-box exercise that slows things down or creates unnecessary barriers. I'd like to be known for making security practical and accessible-something anyone can engage with, without feeling lost in technical jargon.

I also hope I've supported others along the way -especially those who, like me, didn't take a traditional path into cybersecurity. I know how intimidating it can feel to enter this space without a technical background, as if you don't speak the same language as everyone else. If I've been able to help people build confidence, find their place, and see that cybersecurity thrives on diverse skills-not just technical expertise-that's something I'd be truly proud of.

Emma Mackenzie

We see you as a role model because of all the amazing work you do in the cybersecurity industry! Tell the readers a little about you and your cybersecurity career to date.

My career in cybersecurity began a little differently from others. I am a career changer who went from Hairdresser/Makeup Artist to Information Security Governance Analyst after completing an intensive 16-week full time cybersecurity security bootcamp, then gained my promotion to Information Security Governance Specialist within my first 18 months.

I never thought a job could ever become a passion, but that is exactly what this industry is to me. I have definitely thrown myself straight in at the deep end by attending and speaking at industry events about my career change, with the hopes of inspiring hiring managers into giving others like me that chance of showing what they have to offer. I am also part of the WiCyS UK&I leadership team, leading and supporting some of our partnerships and events, and I have recently just accepted the role of Internal Operations Lead, something I am extremely grateful for and proud of.

One of my favourite things about this industry is the fantastic people I get to meet. Walking into a crowded room of strangers is pretty daunting but there will always be a friendly face ready to chat and make you feel welcome and as that has always been the reception I have received; I try to make sure I am now that person able to offer that comfort to anyone looking a little lost in those situations.

Life is not always straightforward. Share a challenge you have faced which has impacted your career, and if you can, what you did to get past it.

During the beginning of my second year in my role, everything started to feel like it was falling apart. I had been told my role was at risk of redundancy and my Gran had just been diagnosed with cancer. In those early months I made every effort to focus on the positives that were also happening for me. I had just been nominated for the 'Most Inspiring Women in Cyber' awards and had also been selected for the 'Empowering Women To Lead Cyber Security' programme.

This programme became a massive support for me in more ways than I could ever thank my cohort and the Empowering-You team for. On my first day, my gran had gone in to hospital for her first chemo session and by the end of my second day she had suffered a stroke. She passed away the day before my Empowering-You graduation just twelve weeks later, but with all of the amazing support I had received from the people at work and the Empowering-You team, I was able to attend my graduation and deliver my presentation along with my team.

Throughout this time, I had made the decision not to let the redundancy worry get in my way and to make the most of every opportunity I had at that time. That's when the chance to throw myself into some more challenging work came around which then ultimately helped me gain my promotion. The day I told my Gran I had gotten the promotion was the last time I got to see her really smile and I will forever be grateful for that memory. I would say that all of these things impacted my career and it could have all gone in a completely different direction had I not used work as a distraction to the things going on in my personal life.

We think you shine! Share a moment in your career where you felt you turned a corner and you have achieved something you're proud of.

The thing I am most proud of in my career (aside from my promotion) is my work in setting up the 'Cyber Diverse IT' community internally at work. It started off as an idea from my colleague Erin who wanted to build a safe space for women in cybersecurity and technology roles and has grown into a committee of 8. We share monthly blog posts internally on thought-provoking subjects such as burn out, the gender pay gap, menopause and the 'lift as you climb' mindset, and one of our 2024 highlights was hosting a Q&A session with Chris Woodcock on our experiences with the Empowering-You programme. We have lots planned for 2025 and have even managed to secure sponsorship from senior leadership.

When you're old and grey, and you look back over what we are sure will be an epic cybersecurity career, what would you like your legacy to look like? Is there anything in particular you'd like to have accomplished?

As someone still quite early in my career, I don't have a particular career goal. I am still finding my feet and working out what I enjoy and what I don't, but if I was to leave any kind of legacy, it would be one of empowerment and inspiration. Something I am extremely passionate about, is encouraging and supporting people making a career change and supporting women and other underrepresented minorities in their information and cybersecurity security careers. If my career change story encourages just one hiring manager to give someone a chance, then I know I will have made a massive difference to someone's life. I look forward to developing my own career further whilst inspiring and mentoring others.

Bharti Lim

We see you as a role model because of all the amazing work you do in the cybersecurity industry! Tell the readers a little about you and your cybersecurity career to date.

I started working in security about 18 years ago, almost straight after university. I did a module in security in my final year, and it had me hooked at that point, and I knew what I wanted to do. I have worked in a number of roles starting in IT Support, making my move into security as a Firewall Logfile Analyst (before SIEM became a thing and everything was still manual), to a Support Engineer, Consultant, Sales Engineer/Pre-Sales, and eventually to where I am now as Security Strategy Manager.

Life is not always straightforward. Share a challenge you have faced which has impacted your career, and if you can, what you did to get past it.

Starting in this space 18 years ago, the world was very different in terms of the number of women in security, especially in technical roles, the senior roles they would go into, and how inclusive organisations were. A number of times, I left the office crying and wondering if this was the type of career where I could be successful. It's lucky that I have a 'I'm going to prove you wrong' attitude, and decided to do exactly that and stuck it out. I am proud to say that my career has gone on to be more successful than those men that made sexist jibes at me and told me I should not be in security.

One of the hardest things for me was coming back from maternity leave, where typically people doing my role were men and would only have had two weeks off. They were not familiar with the process of bringing a woman back into security after a year out. A lot can happen in the security world in one year, and navigating the onboarding back into work was not handled the way it should have been. Again, at this point I did consider if being a Mum and working in this type of role would work for me, and I did nearly leave security as a career. I was very fortunate to find a role at a company after my second stint of maternity leave that worked for me. I have used that opportunity to help me progress my career in a place that wants me to succeed, and where I can give back, so other women in tech do not think their careers will be limited by starting families. I want to make sure they have doors opened up for them if they want them, and ensure they feel empowered that there are opportunities for senior roles available to them.

We think you shine! Share a moment in your career where you felt you turned a corner and you have achieved something you're proud of.

For me, it was the personal move of not standing behind everyone during my career but standing alongside, and sometimes even at the front with my views and knowledge. I always felt my voice was not important, but now my view is valued and appreciated. In my technical career, there are a number of things that I can be proud of, but the impact of those vs the impact of how I now see myself and others do too, is my biggest achievement.

When you're old and grey, and you look back over what we are sure will be an epic cybersecurity career, what would you like your legacy to look like? Is there anything in particular you'd like to have accomplished?

I would like to think I will have encouraged more women into this career from all the school outreach and mentoring work I do, and helped those already in this career to believe they can hold those senior positions. I hope some of these girls will go on to remember that there once was a woman who came into their school and did a talk that changed their career trajectory.

I would also like to have made an impact on the men in this field, to know that women are just as, if not more, capable of achieving the same things. I hope my message about the 'power of the network' will become something everyone from underrepresented groups takes advantage of and uses to help them achieve their goals and be successful. I would like to also have made an impact where I work in changing the way we do things in the security area.

Rafat Yewande Alabelewe

We see you as a role model because of all the amazing work you do in the cybersecurity industry! Tell the readers a little about you and your cybersecurity career to date.

I started my cybersecurity journey through the CyberLearner community after initially not getting into the CyberGirls Fellowship. Undeterred, I trained as a GRC (governance, risk, and compliance) professional with CyberLearner, which strengthened my foundation in cybersecurity. Later, I had the opportunity to join the CyberGirls Fellowship, where I specialised as an Incident Response Analyst. I am passionate about promoting digital hygiene, and helping aspiring cybersecurity professionals navigate their journey. My long-term goal is to help organisations safeguard themselves from cybersecurity-attacks by implementing strong security measures and fostering a culture of cybersecurity resilience.

Life is not always straightforward. Share a challenge you have faced which has impacted your career, and if you can, what you did to get past it.

When I started my cybersecurity journey, I experienced imposter syndrome and was often scared to put myself out there. I doubted whether I truly belonged in the field, which made it difficult to fully embrace opportunities. At the same time, I struggled with balancing my learning alongside other responsibilities. To overcome this, I decided to break my tasks into smaller, manageable bits, allowing me to stay consistent without feeling overwhelmed. Over time, I built confidence in my skills, and learned to trust my growth process. Now, I'm passionate about helping others navigate similar challenges as they start their own cybersecurity journeys.

We think you shine! Share a moment in your career where you felt you turned a corner and you have achieved something you're proud of.

A major turning point in my cybersecurity journey was getting into the CyberGirls Fellowship. It gave me access to valuable resources that deepened my understanding of cybersecurity, and provided mentorship that guided my growth. One of my proudest moments was receiving the BTL1 voucher, successfully passing the exam, and earning a gold coin.

When you're old and grey, and you look back over what we are sure will be an epic cybersecurity career, what would you like your legacy to look like? Is there anything in particular you'd like to have accomplished?

When I look back on my cybersecurity career, I want my legacy to be one of impact and awareness. I hope to have played a significant role in promoting cybersecurity hygiene, ensuring that individuals and organisations understand the importance of protecting their digital assets. I also want to be remembered for helping organisations stay secure by implementing strong cybersecurity measures and fostering a culture of resilience.

Sophie Powell

We see you as a role model because of all the amazing work you do in the cybersecurity industry! Tell the readers a little about you and your cybersecurity career to date.

I knew from a young age that I would like a career in cybersecurity security and was accepted into a brilliant university course that allowed me to explore many different areas of the field. Alongside becoming a co-founder of CyberWomen Groups C.I.C., I went on to complete a rotational graduate scheme in a cybersecurity security consultancy. I am now a Junior Cyber Consultant with the same company, gaining experience in a range of areas, with a manager that I consider to be one of the most inspiring women I have met.

Life is not always straightforward. Share a challenge you have faced which has impacted your career, and if you can, what you did to get past it.

In setting up CyberWomen Groups C.I.C. at the age of 21, I gained the title of 'Director' very early on in my career. The stereotypical Director tends to be considerably further along in their career than I was, so predictably this was met with a handful of unkind comments and raised eyebrows. I learnt very quickly that not everyone is going to like you, just because you're helping the community and pursuing something you think everyone else would be passionate about too.

Despite this, the overwhelming support we have received from so many others made this challenge much easier to tackle. It certainly made me much more resilient, a quality I have found to be valuable in many areas of life!

We think you shine! Share a moment in your career where you felt you turned a corner and you have achieved something you're proud of.

One of the proudest moments of my career was our first conference as CyberWomen@Warwick. The core team, six of us, made our closing remarks, saw our final attendees out and looked at each other in disbelief. We had over 250+ attendees, cold-called all our speakers and met some incredible role-models in the field.

Between the squealing, hugging, and exhaustion, it was one of the most rewarding materialisations of hard work I have experienced, with some of the best peers I could have wished for.

When you're old and grey, and you look back over what we are sure will be an epic cybersecurity career, what would you like your legacy to look like? Is there anything in particular you'd like to have accomplished?

I'd love to be remembered as somebody approachable, kind, and warm in this industry. From my experiences as a student, I know speaking to people with well-respected job titles can be nerve-wracking, and sometimes met with resistance.

If I can contribute to a community that prioritises growth, warmth, and encouraging confidence in our workforce, remembering we are all only human, I'd be extremely proud.

Bronwyn Boyle

We see you as a role model because of all the amazing work you do in the cybersecurity industry! Tell the readers a little about you and your cybersecurity career to date.

I started my career as a Software Engineer, cutting Java code and running technology delivery projects during the first wave of digital banking services during the DotCom era. At the time, developers received very little support or training on security: it was seen as someone else's problem and often bolted on at the end of the development lifecycle. This didn't sit well with me, so I took time to upskill, with a MSc. in Security & Forensic Computing.

This marked my pivot to a career in security. Since then, I've been privileged to work across all security disciplines in a broad range of organisations, from start-ups and scale-ups to global financial institutions and regulatory bodies. I'm currently CISO at a payments FinTech company called PPRO: we enable businesses to offer online and mobile customers access to trusted, preferred local payment methods around the world. I also lead on secure, ethical AI enablement for PPRO, and at an industry level.

I have a passion for security, innovation, and improving alignment to address security and fraud-related threats. I'm also committed to driving diversity, and improving mental health in cybersecurity. As a Non-Executive Director and Board Advisor, I support a number of FinTechs and RegTechs on security and privacy, strategy, and product development.

Life is not always straightforward. Share a challenge you have faced which has impacted your career, and if you can, what you did to get past it.

I had a bad horse-riding accident and broke my back, so I've had to manage chronic pain for many years. It was very difficult to get a handle on in the early days and nearly derailed my career. After many years of medical interventions, I spent time with the fabulous folks at St Guys & Thomas Pain Clinic. I learned invaluable skills and mental approaches to manage my pain, build resilience and practice acceptance.

It's made me so aware that many folks are managing hidden health issues day-to-day that can impact their wellbeing, performance, and mindset, so it's super important to be empathetic and kind. I'm very grateful for the amazing support I got during my most difficult time (shout-out to Stephen Bonner, now being brilliant at the UK Information Commissioner's Office) and am determined to pay this forward!

We think you shine! Share a moment in your career where you felt you turned a corner and you have achieved something you're proud of.

It was a privilege to drive and support industry-wide initiatives, including the implementation of Confirmation of Payee to combat payment fraud, development of resources to empower Small to Medium Enterprises to improve their security and fraud posture, and building trusted collaboration and intelligence sharing communities across the open banking ecosystem. The security and fraud prevention measures we established gave consumers and businesses confidence in the system, reinforcing trust in digital finance. This was particularly important during COVID-19, when Open Banking became a lifeline for many individuals and small businesses needing rapid access to more flexible credit, or needing help with financial management. It was incredible to be part of this journey, and to oversee significant growth and adoption of open banking. I'm excited to see how it continues to evolve as the UK moves towards Open Finance and beyond!

When you're old and grey, and you look back over what we are sure will be an epic cybersecurity career, what would you like your legacy to look like? Is there anything in particular you'd like to have accomplished?

I'd love my legacy to reflect a more safer, fairer, more transparent, and resilient online world, populated by happy, healthy, confident online citizens. cybersecurity isn't just about stopping threats - it's also about enabling people to live and work online without fear and with confidence. We're living in a time where cybersecurity and fraud threats are escalating, AI-fuelled misinformation and psychological manipulation is on the rise, and where the digital divide is driving social fragmentation and leaving people behind. I'd like to look back and know I helped to make the digital world more trusted, trustworthy and equitable.

Chapter 5 - Closing Words

A big thank you to the incredible role models who shared their journeys and experiences so openly with us all. It's not an easy thing to do, and so we are very grateful!

As you can see, there are so many roles, experiences, excitement, and challenges that come with working in cybersecurity. Interestingly, many of the stories our writers shared could be applied to lots of different industries, so maybe this isn't just a cybersecurity situation?

Anyhow, these role models are waiting for your LinkedIn requests, your messages, and your connections! If you are wanting to build out your network, these are the perfect individuals to add to it. We chose them for their resiliencies, their passion, motivations, and accomplishments. They are the future of the cybersecurity industry.

6 STOP RUNNING FROM YOUR PERSONAL BRAND

What comes to mind when you hear the words personal brand? A shudder, perhaps? For most of us, it's a mix of buzzwords, curated LinkedIn feeds, and the constant pressure to look like you have your ducks completely in a row. Maybe you're rolling your eyes right now, thinking, 'I'm not an influencer.' I don't need a brand. Or perhaps you've dabbled in building one but found the whole concept overwhelming, even inauthentic. We know, we've been there.

Here's the thing: whether you like it or not, you do have a personal brand...we all do! It's not about selfies or hashtags; it's about the way people perceive you, and all of your wonderful qualities. Your values, your strengths, and the impact you have on those around you. As we've spoken about before, in a world of digital first-impressions, opinions are formed in second, and running from this truth doesn't make it disappear. In fact, it only ensures that someone else defines your narrative for you.

This chapter isn't about turning you into a walking billboard for yourself and your company, or pushing you to create a version of yourself that feels fake. Instead, personal branding is about embracing your authenticity and understanding that your personal brand already exists in how you treat others, the work you produce, and the legacy you're creating. So, stop running. We'll unpack the fears, tackle the misconceptions, and uncover the benefits that come from embracing your brand with purpose and clarity.

You've been building your personal brand all along. We're going to tell you how to take ownership of it.

What are the important things to know when building out my personal brand?

We're not going to beat around the bush. Most of us don't actually know what a personal brand is. We've seen a definite surge of activity around personal branding in the last year, making it feel like a 'new' concept, when really, it's just a new name for something you probably already have... a reputation (kind of).

The blend of your personality, values, experiences, and abilities that influences how other people see you makes up your personal brand. It's not only about your career accomplishments. It's also about your personality, communication style, and the influence you have on the people and environments around you. Consider it more deliberate and comprehensive than your reputation. One way to think of is it -what do people think of when they hear your name? They think of you (your personal brand), which is the narrative you convey through your choices, behaviours, and online/offline presence. Everyone has a personal brand, whether they are aware of it or not, and that it is a constantly changing part of their life and work.

A successful personal brand is built on the foundation of sincerity and clarity. Understanding who you are and what you stand for deeply is the first step in creating one that resonates. For example, Amelia has formed an element of her personal branding on being passionate about supporting Charities and Small Businesses with cybersecurity, and people know her for that brand. Spend some time thinking about your defining characteristics, strengths, and core values; what matters to you? These are what set your brand apart and help people remember it. Since people are drawn to individuals who are sincere and consistent in who they are, authenticity is particularly crucial.

This is why your brand must truly be a reflection of you. In the short term, pretending to be someone you're not may seem enticing, but it frequently results in fatigue, misalignment, and eventually a decline in trust of those around you. Being your authentic self ensures the sustainability of your own brand and helps you to facilitate and maintain genuine connections with others.

What makes you stand out can often be what you feel makes you 'useful' in your community. Determine your niche by thinking about what you are genuinely enthusiastic about, and how your knowledge or abilities meet a particular demand. The junction of your passion, your skills, and what other people value should be reflected in your specialisation. An example could be your cybersecurity specialism itself, such as Incident Response, maybe it's your ability to mentor or coach, or maybe it's your skillset to break down cybersecurity topics. Whatever makes you tick should feed into your brand.

Another consideration, when building your brand, is knowing who your target audience is. Whether they are prospective employers, clients, or the general public, it's important to tailor your content and messaging to cover some of their expectations, interests, and needs. That's how you will appeal to them and build up the brand! Your brand continuously conveys your worth, and so representing yourself appropriately, will draw in the right opportunities and build trust with your connections and network.

You've defined your personal brand -what comes next? Consistency is key to reinforcing your identity, and again building trust. This applies not only to your messaging, but also to the visuals, tone, and overall presence you maintain across different platforms and interactions. Whether you're engaging on social media, networking in person, or presenting your work, your communication and actions should align with the values and image you aim to project. Consistency doesn't mean being inflexible, it's about ensuring that your brand feels cohesive and authentic, no matter the medium or situation.

Speaking of communication channels, we can't hide away from the fact that our personal brands are most commonly communicated in a professional setting via LinkedIn. We know that our social media profiles are often the first impressions others form of us, especially professionally. We call it the window to the professional soul! Again, it's essential that these platforms accurately reflect the brand you want to present. Spend some time carefully selecting content to make sure it reflects your values, area of expertise, and desired public persona. On the other hand, take time reviewing older posts and connections, and if they do not fit with who you are, remove them (we all have digital pasts, some of which we might regret).

Make the most of your profile by showcasing your personality, insights, and distinct viewpoint in addition to your accomplishments. Being active in communicating with your audience by taking part in pertinent discussions and distributing valuable content maintains consistency, whilst creating opportunities for you to meaningfully interact with others. An example when we relate this to cybersecurity could be posting in mentoring opportunities, events or, interesting articles in cybersecurity groups via LinkedIn such as WiCyS (Women in Cybersecurity) or CyberWomen Groups CIC. This gains visibility, shows who you are and what you represent, and can help with networking building.

We often see personal branding as a very individual process, but a personal brand isn't something you build alone. It's shaped by the relationships you cultivate and the way you interact with others. Making connections within the wider industry, such as working with peers, or interacting with mentors all have an impact on how people see you. They help to shape your own personal brand.

Focus on sharing your skills and experience freely and widely, in order to develop a powerful and favourable personal brand.

In addition, listen to others to understand what elements of their brands that you also might wish to incorporate into your own, being sure to remain authentic. In listening to others, we encourage you to celebrate the accomplishments of people around you. It is far too easy for us to get caught up in maintaining our own brands, that we forget to celebrate others in the way that we would like to be celebrated. If you see a fellow professional smashing it, give them a 'like', repost it to your account, or private message them. You have nothing to lose and you could end up making their day as well as affiliating some fab content with your profile and subsequent brand.

Much like your goals, an important element of personal branding is flexibility. Your personal brand changes as you go and grow. Your brand should vary as you mature, acquire new experiences, and hone your goals. Review your personal brand on a regular basis, as you would with your goals to make sure it still reflects your passion, values, and abilities as well as the path you wish to take. Being adaptable is essential to maintaining your fundamental identity whilst keeping current and receptive to new opportunities. By embracing this flexibility, your brand may remain genuine, and in line with your audience's demands as well as your own personal development.

I'm finding it hard to identify what my personal brand is. How can I gain greater clarity on this?

As we said above, personality, values, experiences, and abilities add together into forming your personal brand. It boils down to one question- 'what do you want people to think when they hear your name?' This is your outward brand and the driver of your next steps, opportunities, networking moments and how individuals advocate for you and recommend you. This is who you 'are'.

When you're identifying what you want your personal brand to be, we fully get this can be hard. It's not always easy to pinpoint what you do and don't want out there, and also what will add up to a successful career. A fabulous place to therefore start, is by creating a 'joy' list. When you think about your day-to-day life and career, what brings you joy in what you do? What makes you happy and makes you want to do whatever you're doing? The 'joy' list can be anything... but it must consist of items which make you feel... well... joyful! Examples could be:

- I love to speak at schools about online safety
- I love using statistics to prove my point on where to spend IT budget
- I love creating new content for our company website
- I love making difficult cybersecurity jargon or technicalities into accessible content for our customer base
- I love helping charities to be cybersecurity aware
- I love advocating for women to be in the cybersecurity space

The list doesn't have to be endless, but your 'joys' feed into what your personal brand is, or could be. If you took any one of the above bulleted list, and that was forever more in your day-to-day, would that make you happy? If we then got to show that outwardly to the rest of the world, would you have something to share? Could you be a subject matter expert, or simply be able to express interesting information and thought leadership on the item? When we think back to that question, 'what do you want people to think when they hear your name?', knowing what your joys are, and then using that to identify who you are in the field and what you can bring, helps.

Another consideration when trying to identify your personal brand is reflection. We can easily get caught up in working (or surviving), and forget all the amazing things we have done or accomplished. Look through your emails, your career development plans, your 'smug list' (Chapter 4), your peer feedback, and identify moments you have shined. Was it for something you'd like to do more of? Was it for something you do all the time and that you actually enjoy?

Was it an area you'd like future opportunities to be in? Again, reflecting on who you are, where you've been, and therefore what you'd like to carry forward and share via your platforms, can feed into your personal brand and identity.

Personal brand has to be authentic to you. That being said, it can be tailored to supporting a dream or vision that isn't quite 'you' yet. As an example, say you had a career dream of being a Secure System Developer. Whilst you may not be there yet, having a personal brand that has a keen interest and consistent postings in all things penetration testing, secure development lifecycles, agile techniques and the like, could all add up to getting you that role. It demonstrates interest, thought leadership, knowledge. When a recruiter or leader looks at your profile, that's what they will see and that's the kind of related opportunities that will knock at your door. Personal brand isn't just about the now, it's also about the future.

If you're still struggling, there is one final way to identify your personal brand…ask someone! Again, if we reflect back on the question, 'what do you want people to think when they hear your name?' Could you ask that to a mentee, a trusted friend, a colleague? What do they think you're fabulous at or are synonymous with? The results may surprise you, delight you, or maybe even disappoint you. Either way, it can highlight what you are or are not happy with being known for, and furthermore figure out what to dig deeper into or build your outward presence around.

Are awards and industry recognition a big part of personal brand? I am seeing awards everywhere but have never been nominated.

This is a topic in which we differ. If you'd ask Rebecca, she'd say 'we do love a good award or piece of industry recognition! 'However, if you ask Amelia, she'll tell you that there's a raft of secret politics involved. But they aren't easy to come by and sadly (and we hate to see this) there really can be a lot of secret politics involved in bagging a win. Let's drill down into it.

Industry recognition is obviously fantastic. They feed into career progression, personal development, and personal brand. They can be a brilliant way to recognise you and your contribution in industry. We are seeing more and more, 'women-in-cybersecurity' specific awards, which are obviously awesome, but there is something to be said for women not being able to just win and have better representation in the wider cybersecurity awards that consistently take place (a topic for another day). To be eligible for an award, you must be nominated, or self-nominate, into categories that you can evidentially prove you have successfully contributed to and done well in (think 'Role Model of the Year' or 'Best Emerging Researcher'). You typically have to have gone above and beyond and made a fundamental difference. Awards aren't normally just given to anyone for every-day work and accomplishments.

So, to start with, we'll address self-nominations. We can all feel a bit yucky about self-nominations, but actually if you can't advocate for yourself, who can? Not everyone is out there looking for opportunities to nominate colleagues, and even more so specifically hunting out awards to celebrate you. So, if you see something you feel you should be a nominee for, we encourage you to just go for it and self-nominate. Celebrate yourself! Judges do not know how you ended up in any given category and simply just review the entry and evidence. There is no bias behind self-nominating. We actually think it's something you should be proud of.

Nominations can come from anyone in any industry, and there are lots of awards happening, seemingly all of the time. The best way to keep track of what nominations are open and when is by using your LinkedIn. Do your research into key industry awards, and then follow the owners or hosts of those awards on LinkedIn. They will post when the nominations open and you can get populating those forms. Alternatively, many award providers now have an emailing list, so you can sign up to receive notifications and be the first to hear when doors open.

If you do receive a notification and you know someone smashing it, please nominate. It really can make someone's day and give them the pat on the back they deserve. It can also be a springboard into new exciting opportunities for them, something which if they're smashing it, they deserve! So get that nomination in.

Just to touch on process. If a nomination is accepted, there is often a follow up with questions to the nominee. They are normally asked to share what they have done that means they should win, describe situations where they have demonstrated core skills, and typically have to share a bio and headshot. In some cases, there are even panel interviews. Whatever pathway it takes, be sure to have statistics and 'brags' (chapter 4) you can use to show how you shine. In addition, have at least one or two people in your mind who could be a reference for the award panel, should that be required. Statistics, metrics, and clear examples of positive influence, can make a HUGE difference between a nomination and a win. Have them in your front of mind for these kinds of moments.

Now, we mentioned politics. We can't talk about awards without calling it how it is. Many awards are sponsored by organisations, that's how they get the money to run the awards to start with, and it is a business of its own. As a result, there will likely be candidates for awards from these sponsor organisations, which can make the competition that little bit more challenging. Additionally, and we hate to say it, there can sometimes be sway in the judges. Whilst we hope everyone is impartial, the cybersecurity industry really isn't that big and so panels can sometimes be made of familiar faces reviewing a bunch of familiar nominees. Making sure you have a strong, evidenced-backed nomination entry, should squash any 'sway', but just be conscious it may be there, and it isn't your fault.

Whether you become a finalist, a winner, or not, make sure you nod to your nomination via your social profile and add it to your LinkedIn. It adds weight to the fact others are seeing you, and acknowledging you. Finally, whilst awards are often free to enter, typically the event itself isn't. This itself is a barrier to entry and can sometimes take away the buzz. If you are wanting to progress a nomination, it can help to understand what implied costs there could be and also if your organisation would support the cost. You should 100% still do the rest of the process, but it can help with your own expectation setting.

So, that's the need-to-know information. But do awards matter? The answer is, that depends on you, and how much weight you personally put on to them. Will winning an award feed significantly into what you want people to know about you? Is an award part of your identity and image? We feel they are nice-to-haves rather than defining characteristics, but we acknowledge that for some, they cement their contributions in stone. For some, a win can mean finally receiving a grant, getting a promotion, or ticking a box that means they can progress. For others, it is a wholesome moment, where they feel accepted and appreciated. How an award influences your personal brand, is entirely down to you.

All in all, whilst they're nice, awards and industry recognitions don't have to define you or your contributions. If you do feel something similar could help, consider 'recommendations' on your LinkedIn where others can write their experiences of working with you. This in itself has a feel-good factor and still advocates for your contributions and successes. If you feel that you deserve an award then self-nominate, chat up a friend, or keep sending notifications around about the awards event in the hope that someone will put two and two together and nominate you! There are also so many free awards, so cost doesn't have to be a limiting factor if this is a concern (check out awards from IT Guru & Eskenzi PR). Do what makes you smile and feel happy. Just remember, it really isn't the be all and end all.

How can I leverage my personal brand to influence my career pathway?

Leveraging your personal brand in your career means intentionally shaping how others perceive your unique skills, values, and personality so that you can open doors to new opportunities. You may have a personal brand, but how can you use it positively to have a tangible impact on your career?

A personal brand can be complex, but in order to leverage yours, you need to construct your personal brand statement. Think of it a bit like your mission statement. One or two sentences that succinctly and persuasively describe who you are, what you do, and the special value you bring. Similar to the elevator pitch concept that we've discussed previously, it provides a concise overview of your professional identity, and makes it easier for others to comprehend your unique selling points, areas of expertise, and abilities. You may wish to use this in your networking activity, your CV, or as your LinkedIn bio.

Another part of leveraging your personal brand is to have it readily available for whatever you want from your career. Is your LinkedIn in the best possible condition? Is your blog or portfolio ready? Have you got references in mind to support you? Is your CV tailored to an application for the role you're after? Are these refining your personal brand?

As we highlighted previously, personal brand is not static. It evolves and changes, just like the world itself. It is therefore important to keep your personal brand aligned with where you are now, and where you're looking to go. As per our previous example, if you wanted to be in technical testing, having an active social presence, posts, content, and a CV that aligns with that supports outside perception. It shows that you are engaged in the specialism and ready for new opportunities. Always try and be ahead of the curve (we know sometimes easier said than done) and leverage your personal brand, and anything else that adds up to be the awesome person you are... DO IT!

Finally, when it comes to your personal brand, don't be ashamed to use it! Own the brand you created, and don't be shy about it. You have spent time, energy and enthusiasm building your outward facing brand, so be loud and proud in using it to your advantage and to aid your career progression. Not only that but the elements that make up your brand are YOU. Your skills, your community engagements, your beliefs, your ethics, your morals, and your passions. If you need to use that to get a job over the line, do it. Many others simply wouldn't be as shy about embracing it and working such information to their advantage.

Now, to touch on the 'how'. That ball is well and truly in your court. Your brand connects to your accomplishments, contributions, 'smugs' and 'joys' - deciding how much of that you want to share and use to your advantages, is with you and is something you have to be comfortable with. Some individuals prefer to keep elements of their life private, like volunteering or mentoring, and you may be similar. Some people like to catalogue every element of everything they do. Whatever your style, we recommend defining what you're happy to put out there, and how it fits into you succeeding in a career goal. What adds up to you appearing valuable and right for the position? Then use that to 'wiggle' yourself into a mould that fits the career you're after. A final angle to consider is when you are pushing for a promotion or a career change, being able to demonstrate how your brand has changed, maybe even how your brand could better support the business or role objectives, all adds to you being more desirable. Keep an eye on the next promotion opportunity, understand what your career pathway looks like, and be ready to tweak your personal brand to suit those opportunities.

Are there specific platforms and places that I should leverage to share my personal brand?

This is tricky, simply because there are so many out there! The first place we recommend starting is to figure out where your audience lies. Consider:

- Is your brand driven by ambition in more personal or professional spaces?
- What are you wanting to use your brand to accomplish? Is it to create awareness of cybersecurity risk? Is it to influence? Is it to cause change? Is it simply just to put something interesting out?
- What kind of content are you wanting to share? Posts or blogs? Photos or video shorts?

Understanding these can help you identify the appropriate platform or place to shine online. Every platform has a different purpose, and has a different audience as a result, so do your research to identify which one suits your needs and the type of outreach you're wanting to make.

To highlight a few, that hopefully help direct you with these next steps:

- TikTok - Plenty of influencers are using TikTok to make short, sharp videos, and for the purpose of typically influencing or educating. As an example, there are quite a few educators leveraging TikTok to talk to their younger audience about STEM-led topics (GenZ make up 60% of the user base of this platform - something to consider from an audience perspective!). That being said, TikTok is more about your personal space, your interests and trend setting.
- LinkedIn - LinkedIn has a professional vibe. It is a platform designed for the business community, where employees of different backgrounds and experiences can come together. It is used to write posts, and share clips as appropriate, on topics usually related to the corporate world. On occasion, there are more personal styled posts, but really this is a platform for workplace content, careers and industry-led thought leadership.
- Medium - Medium self describes as a 'home for human stories and ideas', and is a platform typically used for writing articles. There is no limitation on what these articles can be about, but writers can establish a space with a profile and add their own content as they see fit. It is fantastic if you have a key vision or set of thoughts that you want to expand on and reference on, particularly on other platforms like LinkedIn.
- X (or Twitter depending on your era) - again, an incredibly influencer led platform, although it is used by organisations including cybersecurity firms to share news and links to content. X is probably the most relaxed of all the platforms we have spoken about so far, where pretty much any kind of

content goes. Depending on the topics you're talking about, this could be a good place to post and even strike up conversations with other 'followers' on hot topics or topics where debate could ensue. Others are using BlueSky as an alternative to X. It has the same functionality, but you may feel more comfortable using it in light of recent political events.

So, a handful there to consider! As you can see, they all have a different energy, purpose and audience type. Consider which platform you'd like to leverage to host your brand and make sure you get the most positive result.

Chapter 6- Closing Words

We totally get that 'personal brand', as a term can feel yucky! It can almost feel inauthentic. But actually, personal brand goes hand in hand with career development, and with future opportunities. It can be leveraged in so many ways to give you a louder, prouder voice in the world of cybersecurity, and even be able to influence not only your next steps, but the cybersecurity vision and industry as a whole.

To end this chapter, we wanted to share some extra resources you could visit when trying to build out your personal brand. It's impossible to list them all, but these are some callout experts who we believe can help. Enjoy!

- She Almighty (shealmighty.com)- Mikaela Jackson, found of She Almighty, is fabulous in so many ways. Taken from her own words-'My mission is to free you from your limitations, expectations, the shoulds, the coulds and the what ifs, so that you can step courageously and confidently into your power, shine bright, thrive and create the impact you are destined to have'. Rebecca herself has benefited from her personal brand advice, having met Mikaela at a workshop many moons ago. An advocate and ally to watch!
- Amelia Sordell - Amelia is a podcaster, speaker, and influencer. She is also the founder of the UK's leading Personal Branding Agency, Klowt. Amelia has a book on Amazon called 'The Personal Branding Playbook: Turn Your Personality Into Your Competitive Advantage' (link in the appendices). This book can really help in figuring out who you want to be, and how to get there!

7 MAKING LEMONADE OUT OF CAREER LEMONS

It would be wonderful if every career path were a smooth journey. But for most of us, the ride includes unexpected detours. Be it disappointments, layoffs, stalled promotions, or work environments that zap our motivation, there will always be something that impacts us. When life hands you these career lemons, you have two choices: stay stuck in bitterness or roll up your sleeves and whip up some lemonade (cringe, we know).

This chapter is all about embracing proactive, empowering decision-making that turns setbacks into stepping stones for future success. From volunteering to blogging, there are so many opportunities outside of your workplace that can be transformative to expand your network, boost your confidence, and build credibility in your field. These activities not only help you grow professionally, but also reignite your passion and sense of purpose. We'll dive in and explore how to harness these strategies to thrive, no matter what curveballs your career journey throws at you.

I feel I am being treated differently because I'm a woman. How can I address this?

We hate that this is a question that we have to address, and it's so disappointing that in 2025 this is still an issue (and sadly one we don't see going away soon).

Bias refers to holding a prejudiced perspective towards an individual or group, which can manifest as an inclination for or against them. Such partiality can influence or cloud our choices and responses. Having such entrenched opinions and bias can cause us to disregard factual evidence and alternative perspectives, and behave in a way that ultimately leads to individuals feeling dismissed and unincluded. There are enough types of bias in the world that we could write an entirely new book about them, but we're going to explore the key bias type we see in the workplace as women…gender bias. Firstly, we want to make note of the fact that bias can be conscious or unconscious, and are formed through our life experiences. This is a sad reality that needs to change.

So, what is gender bias? Gender bias involves treating individuals differently based on their gender, often through assumptions about which genders are better suited for certain roles. While it can affect anyone, it most commonly targets women. Being treated differently can look and feel very different dependent on the circumstance, but when we relate it to the workplace, it could be as simple as always being made to take the minutes or always make the guests cups of tea, even though you, as a woman, are not junior or below any of your other counterparts in the space. It's slight, but it's there. Another more concerning example may be being passed over for job roles or opportunities, for working cybersecurity incidents or maybe travelling because you 'have kids', despite the fact that your male counterparts are parents too. It is subtle and it is complicated, but if you are a victim of bias, it is something that will make you feel uncomfortable and alone. Gender bias causes self-doubt and can make you feel that you stick out, or are unworthy of certain opportunities and tasks. It hurts and it is wrong.

It is important we recognise the difference between bias and discrimination. Discrimination is where a person is treated unfairly because of who they are or because they possess certain characteristics, which ties closely into prejudice. Protected characteristics under The Equality Act 2010 include age, gender, race, disability, religion, pregnancy and maternity, sexual orientation, gender reassignment, and marriage or civil partnership. Bias refers to an unfair inclination that can influence a person's judgment or decisions. Discrimination happens when these biases lead to actions that unfairly treat individuals or groups differently. It's important to draw a clear line here: if you are experiencing any form of sexual harassment, racial discrimination, or discrimination related to a disability, seek immediate support. Contact your HR department, leadership team, or Citizens Advice. You can also report it to your local police. Stop reading, and take action now!

Another area surrounding bias for us to briefly touch on is how gender bias is present in the technology used in our own industry. If we consider artificial intelligence as an example, this has been shown to have baked-in biases. An article by IBM highlighted how AI and its knowledge was driven by ingested data, and with that in mind, can 'absorb the biases of society that can be quietly embedded in the mountains of data they're trained on.' We know for fact so many of us are using AI capabilities both professionally and organisationally, so it is troubling to know it can have an inherently biased perception, and therefore, outputs.

On a wider scale, we can consider how bias impacts the industry on the whole. Given our workforces are unrepresentative of the world we live in (still skewed heavily towards men), our biases may hinder our ability to understand threats. Threat management is a core pillar of cybersecurity, but if we approach it from the narrow perspective of a small portion of the population, we risk overlooking a wealth of potential solutions. That's why diversity of thought is essential.

If you feel you are a victim of workplace bias, harassment or discrimination, there are several considerations to make and steps to take to start to unravel the discomfort. Primarily, a good way to tackle bias is to speak with a witness. If you have been in a meeting or a situation where you feel that you were treated differently as a result of bias, and there was someone present who could be a trusted sounding board, ask them what they think. It doesn't have to be as direct as, 'do you think X was treating me differently?', but instead be, 'do you think it was odd/strange/unusual that I was asked to do the minutes again? It made me feel XYZ.' A secondary perspective can help in understanding of the situation, and how to plan your course of action.

We are both believers in second chances. Some individuals simply do not realise that they have been biased in their choices and behaviours, largely when unconscious bias is at play. If you do feel comfortable and able, there is something to be said for taking the individual to one side and 'calling it out'. Please, however, only do this if you feel safe and able to do so. Never put yourself in a dangerous, volatile, or unpredictable situation. If you do want to have this conversation, we recommend a structured approach, detailing your experience, and consider having an ally present if it would help you to feel supported, such as your line manager.

You should focus on highlighting what happened, how it made you feel, and what you would prefer them to do in the future. This can happen via email, or face-to-face in a space with adequate privacy. You will likely find that the individual is absolutely mortified at their actions, that it wasn't intentional and that they'll be more conscious of the biases that impact their choices moving forward. Alternatively, be prepared that the individual may dismiss your comments and instead carry on as they were - This is where we'd advise you to consult with your Human Resources (HR) representative.

If you have made unsuccessful attempts to resolve the bias, or if it escalates into discrimination or harassment, you must talk to your HR department. You should not, and do not, deserve to be treated in this way, and you deserve help. Document evidence that incidents have been happening with dates, times and witnesses, and speak to a professional. HR processes can be arduous, and make you feel diminished or that it's 'not worth it', but we'd like to remind you to stand your ground. We'd also encourage you to remain open-minded to the perspectives of others as they try to support you. If you feel dissatisfied with the outcome, do not walk away, rather, keep seeking solutions. You deserve to be treated fairly and as an equal.

Finally, if you think you've spotted bias in the workplace, our recommendation is to be an authentic ally. Speak to the individual and ask how they're feeling. They may not want to talk about it, but knowing someone has seen a negative behaviour and wants to support can be the difference between feeling alone and knowing you have an advocate. On the other hand, the person may be incredibly grateful that someone else spotted it too, encouraging them to take the necessary steps to reduce the bias. You may also need to assess whether you need to call the individual who demonstrated bias out directly. This is a judgment call based on the preference of the victim, so really think carefully before making any reactive decisions.

It is all our responsibility to ensure we work in a collaborative, supportive and unbiased way. Think about the way you're speaking, how you're working, your taskings and leadership styles, and do what you can to ensure everyone has a fruitful, fair and equal seat at the table.

I'm worried I'm stagnating, and losing interest in the whole industry. To try and combat that I'm considering volunteering. Is that a good idea?

After spending a considerable amount of time in a business or an industry you formerly found thrilling, it's quite common to feel as though you're at a standstill or are fading away from it. The initial passion that drew you to the field may occasionally be overshadowed by the pressure to continuously perform and reach goals. Daily chores might become monotonous, and you may start to wonder if you're still making progress or, even if you belong. We've both been there.

When that happens, it's good to be proactive and look into strategies to rekindle your passion and remind yourself of why you chose this course of action. Volunteering is a fantastic method to accomplish that. Contributing time and effort to a nonprofit, grassroots project, or charitable cause not only benefits others, but also offers a chance for both professional and personal development. Volunteering can provide a welcome change of pace by letting you venture outside of your daily routine, gain a fresh perspective on your field, and rediscover a feeling of purpose that may have waned over time.

First and foremost, volunteering can be a great opportunity to strengthen your existing talents, or learn new ones in a relaxed setting. For example, if you want to improve your leadership skills, you could offer to lead a small group of people in planning community activities or events. Because the emphasis is on group development and service rather on rigid corporate goals, having that duty in a volunteer setting seems more motivating than daunting. It can be life-changing to look for a volunteer position in a nonprofit that needs your creative or technical skills, such as digital marketing, web design, data analysis, or project management, if your current role doesn't completely use them. You contribute to a cause you support and acquire practical experience, which might rekindle your passion for the daily duties of your regular employment. Additionally, volunteering frequently exposes you to situations that call for creativity and flexibility, which boosts your self-confidence. You can break free from any sense of professional stagnation by engaging in this positive cycle.

Second, in the midst of a profit-driven workplace, volunteer work often offers a sense of purpose that might have been forgotten. When every project at your day job is evaluated by revenue targets, efficiency measures, or stakeholder satisfaction, it's easy to grow discouraged or cynical. Even if those are legitimate worries, they can occasionally overshadow the more profound motivations for entering your field in the first place, such as creativity, innovation, or the desire to have a significant influence. You can get back in touch with the driving forces that initially motivated you by identifying with a cause that speaks to you personally. Volunteering serves as a reminder that your skills, abilities, and efforts may truly benefit others, often more immediately and visibly than in a business environment. You might have believed that flame was out, but witnessing directly how your contributions assist an underfunded organisation, help a suffering community, or make someone's day might rekindle it. You may then be inspired to look for more interesting tasks or suggest innovations at work that are consistent with your basic beliefs as a result of this revitalised feeling of purpose. When Amelia started CybAid, it was to help others, and cybersecurity was the vessel in which that could be done with her expertise.

From our own experience, we know that volunteering exposes you to situations that you might not normally encounter, which expands your horizons. You can learn about viewpoints, problems, and solutions that exist outside of your typical bubble by getting to know new people, whether they are fellow volunteers, beneficiaries, or local community members. It's simple to become mired in the echo chamber of your team, or even sector at work. Conversely, volunteering may be a dynamic crash course in empathy and open-mindedness, encouraging you to observe problems from different perspectives.

This exposure can stimulate your ability to think creatively and solve problems, particularly if you're encountering problems that are rarely addressed in your regular work. Something you may not have considered, is how volunteering roles, and the people you meet, can broaden your professional network in unexpected ways, because they frequently have a variety of experiences and skill sets. Friendships or professional connections may open up new job avenues for you; you may find a hidden interest in your area or even think about changing careers. You never know when a friendly chat at a charity event over the weekend can lead to a chance to work together on a fascinating new project, or obtain a job that sparks your interest in the field again.

Perhaps an obvious one, but volunteering provides a respite from the routine of your job, which can greatly improve your mood. Even while they are essential, routine workloads can stifle creativity and lead to a downward spiral of boredom or self-doubt. You can mentally decompress by doing something selfless, and working in an environment where helping others comes before hitting targets or making the most money. It's an opportunity to get back in touch with yourself, consider what drives you, and assess your long-term objectives free of typical stresses. Actually, looking forward to your volunteer obligation can help you cope with work-related stress by diverting your attention to something constructive and fulfilling. In your everyday work, this mental reset frequently results in more energy and sharper thinking, which makes it simpler to take on challenging tasks or conceive novel ideas. You can develop resilience by venturing beyond your comfort zone. Every time you adjust to the demands of volunteer work, you improve your capacity to deal with change and uncertainty in other spheres of your life.

Lastly, it's critical to keep in mind that volunteering doesn't require a significant time investment in order to have an impact. The key thing is to give consistently as much as you can, whether you commit to a long-term position at a local organisation, or participate in short-term community projects when you can. Even a few hours on the weekends may make a big difference, not just for the organisation you're helping, but also for your personal sense of fulfilment and future professional outlook. If you're not sure where to begin, look into local community centres or online volunteer platforms to identify causes that fit your values, interests, and skill sets. Remember that organisations can greatly benefit from your professional background and industry understanding!

I've had a knock to my confidence but I want to start putting my ideas out there. How can I start writing articles without feeling like an imposter?

When your confidence has been shaken and you become cautious about sharing your ideas with the public, it may be frightening. We know that knocks in confidence can come from a variety of sources, and often, at the most inconvenient moments. Imposter syndrome can appear and convince us that our voices are unimportant or that our ideas aren't real. However, it's crucial to keep in mind that everyone struggles with these uncertainties occasionally, particularly when stepping outside of their comfort zones. If we relate this to writing an article, it's a bold, visible move. Writing articles and posting them on public forums like Medium or LinkedIn is bold, which in itself is inherently frightening for a lot of us.

Nevertheless, these writing or blogging spaces are there to promote dialogue, information sharing, and the sharing of viewpoints, none of which necessitates that you be a 'perfect' expert. In actuality, relatable experiences and candid comments tend to stir up a deeper emotional response in readers than pieces that sound too formal or cold. Remember that you are the only one with your path, difficulties, and observations. It will be simpler to believe in the worth of your voice if you embrace your sincerity rather than attempting to project an air of mastery. Even if you are unsure of your qualifications, remember that every bit of information you contribute can inspire someone, start a conversation, or provide a new perspective on a well-known subject.

A useful tactic is to start small and specific when you're ready to write, especially if you're feeling unsure. Focus on one aspect of a topic that you are familiar with rather than trying to write a huge, comprehensive piece that addresses every facet of it. Perhaps you've finished a project at work and gained useful knowledge about time management or teamwork. Maybe you have a notion of what an intriguing trend in your industry means for professionals in your field because you have studied it. You can eliminate the pressure to be an expert by concentrating on a single, distinct subject. This focussed strategy not only makes your writing more coherent, but it also lessens the possibility that the size of your piece would overwhelm you. After deciding on a topic, list the main ideas you wish to cover in the article. Consider this outline as a trusted road map that will help you get from one place to another without letting you get lost or veer off course. Be adaptable throughout the process; if new ideas come to mind while you're writing, give them space, but keep your primary goal in mind as well. Outlines are frameworks designed to help you keep your ideas organised, not strict contracts.

Doing some preliminary research to support your viewpoint and boost your confidence may also be beneficial. But take caution not to become permanently locked in 'research mode.' We can be deceived by imposter syndrome into believing that we require further information or credentials before we can discuss a subject. In actuality, presenting a viewpoint or insight doesn't always require an in-depth understanding of the topic; occasionally, your own experiences and noticed trends can have an equally powerful influence. For your own development, consistency is more important than perfection. Therefore, if you are concerned that you are not 'ready', keep in mind that regular publication of smaller, iterative works can result in a more dynamic writing journey rather than a never-ending search for the ideal time to release a masterpiece. As your confidence grows, you'll be able to expand on your current points, strengthen your arguments, and even go back and look at past concepts from new angles.

When you're prepared to present your work to the world, think about doing it slowly by picking a setting that seems a little more comfortable or encouraging. Because LinkedIn frequently connects you with friends, mentors, and coworkers who are aware of your professional experience, it might be an excellent starting point for this. They will have a tendency to provide supportive or constructive criticism. Also, in a work-related setting, LinkedIn's audience frequently focuses on leadership insights, industry trends, professional development, and personal improvement. You will therefore have a higher chance of reaching people who are actually interested in what you have to say if your material is in line with those subjects. It can be really comforting to get early responses from a network that includes people who know you personally.

Medium might be a great choice if you want to talk about themes that aren't strictly professional or if your topics might appeal to a wider or more diversified audience. Many subjects are covered by Medium's writers and users, including entrepreneurship, parenting, art, technology, and personal writings. Supportive groups that may be more receptive than you anticipate can be found by joining relevant Medium publications or following tags that align with your interests. Low interaction early on doesn't mean you're a bad writer; it just means it takes time to develop a following. Everyone begins somewhere, and it's common to make small progress, particularly as you hone your writing technique and gain confidence in expressing your ideas.

Reflection, both before and after publishing, is another effective strategy for combating imposter syndrome. Ask yourself, 'What am I trying to communicate, and who do I hope will find it useful?', before publishing an article. Some of the stress can be relieved by turning your attention from yourself to your audience. You'll shift your focus from self-evaluation, 'is my writing good enough?', to an external viewpoint: 'will someone benefit from reading this?' You can rediscover the worth of your own work with the aid of such a mental shift. A common strategy for overcoming imposter syndrome is to distinguish constructive, unbiased criticism from critical or unrelated self-talk.

Before you share your work broadly, it might also be beneficial to get input from a smaller group of friends or trusted peers. More specialised, individualised insights can be gleaned via a mentor, a small group of like-minded peers, or even a private critique group. They could point out places where you need clarification, or help you in identifying areas where you undervalue your own level of experience. By taking into consideration these issues prior to its debut, you'll feel more equipped to deal with public response. Sometimes all it takes to get you to publish your work is the knowledge that a small group of individuals who value your thoughts have already given their blessing.

Above all, make an effort to avoid letting anyone set you back or let an unfavourable opinion dictate how you view your talents. Particularly after a loss, confidence is rarely restored by a single victory, but rather by consistent work and small wins. Each item you publish is a step towards regaining your confidence. Understand that it's quite natural to experience some anxiety whenever you release a new work; in fact, that uneasiness is frequently an indication that you're developing as a writer and stretching your boundaries.

I have been at my organisation for a long time now, and I think I've reached the end of the road. I'm just not enjoying it. I want to move on but I don't know where to start. Any suggestions?

When you're settled in an organisation, it can be hard to muster up both the energy and the bravery to start hunting for a new job. You are comfortable, you know your firm inside out, you have friends. When you think of a new role, it can entirely fill you with dread and throw out a whirlwind of questions and self-doubts. We acknowledge, and appreciate that. But you're feeling the way you're feeling for a reason. Sometimes it's that you're not progressing or being challenged anymore, sometimes your role just makes you unhappy – so let's drill into some tips and tricks to support job hunting and get you started!

Know your non-negotiables and joy list

It is impossible to job hunt if you don't know what you want. Reflect on your current position- what is working and what isn't? What do you love, not enjoy, utterly hate? What do you actually NEED? Have this documented and available, so you can help direct your search and particularly conversations with recruiters.

Check out the landscape

Before you start hunting, go and have a look at the job landscape and see what opportunities are out there. You may find it better after looking to hold fire for a few weeks, or to go go go! As an example, there are typically less roles being advertised around the end of the financial year, and so you might be better to wait for the new financial year when organisations have budget. Gauge the landscape, maybe even have a chat with a few recruiters to see what's happening, and make a judgment.

Jazz up your CV and online presence

LinkedIn is the window to your professional soul. Make sure your online profile or portfolio is fine-tuned, up-to-date and well presented. It is also time to start thinking about your CV. Recruiters do not typically read past the first page, and so you need to make sure all the key details about you are on there. Examples include:

- Your name, email, mobile and LinkedIn.
- A 'power paragraph' about who you are and what you bring.
- A list of keywords- think tools, skills, attributes, broken apart by commas.
- 3-5 key accomplishments that you can comfortably talk to, and show how you shine!

This needs to be a priority. You can't apply for a role without having these ready.

Put out the feelers

There are many cybersecurity recruitment firms out there, all with fabulous folk ready to understand what you want and find a way to get you there. Some stand out organisations are LT Harper, Adeptis, Trident Search, Experis and Sanderson PLC.

As you put the feelers out, it's also worth exploring your own network. Are there individuals who can help you find a role? Is there anyone working a role that you're really interested in? Reach out to your community and see what's happening! You may end up surprised to find a fabulous opportunity.

Check out your favourite cybersecurity firms and see what they're looking for.

Write a list of organisations you would like to work for. You can identify these just through your own awareness, through network recommendations and through employee reviews of organisations, such as that on Glassdoor. Once you have identified them, sign up to job notifications either on the organisation's direct website, their recruiters, or via their LinkedIn job page.

When you dig into these organisations, have a look at the roles they are actively recruiting for and what the expectations are of their new employees (think hours, location, qualifications, role experience). Try to identify if you have any gaps which you can plug in advance, and build in their asks into your CV, so it's easier for them to see how much of a great fit you would be (should you apply). Additionally, look at the organisation's cultures and values. Make sure they fit with your hopes, and what you would want from an employer.

We hope these tips help. One final note to consider- often when you're feeling the need for a career change, you can end up diving into roles and situations which aren't quite right, just because we are desperate to find 'an out'. With this in mind, it's so important you take your time and really find a role that suits your needs, goals, and ambitions. In some situations, this isn't always possible (like when you've been made redundant), but if you have time and space to make careful considerations, seize that opportunity.

I'm dealing with a toxic work environment, and it's impacting my confidence and performance. What steps can I take to protect myself and move forward?

It can be challenging to deal with a toxic workplace, which leaves you feeling exhausted, demotivated, and doubting your value. However, while the situation may feel overwhelming, there are steps you can take to protect your well-being and regain control. By addressing the toxicity strategically, setting boundaries, and prioritising self-care, you can minimise its impact and create a path forward, whether that involves improving your current situation or leads you to seeking new opportunities.

Recognising the existence of a toxic workplace and how it is impacting your overall mental health is the first and most crucial step in managing it. The early signs of workplace toxicity are frequently subtle, with actions or interactions that appear trivial or inconsequential. These tendencies however, have the potential to worsen over time, having a compounding effect that undermines your sense of wellbeing and career advancement. You can change from feeling like a helpless victim to someone who is actively taking action to regain control by acknowledging the problem. This knowledge keeps you from internalising the issue, or holding yourself responsible for uncontrollable events.

After identifying the toxicity, it's important to thoroughly record any particular instances of negative dynamics or behaviour. Inappropriate remarks, unjust treatment, instances of exclusion, micromanagement, gaslighting, or any other behaviour that compromises a positive work environment could fall under this category. Keeping an objective record is essential because it enables you to examine the problem logically and spot recurring trends, instead of reacting emotionally to specific instances. Make a note of the hours, dates, participants, and details of what happened. You should also include any witnesses who could support your story. For instance, document precisely what was said, how it was said, and the circumstances if a manager publicly chastises you in a degrading way or if a colleague circulates untrue information about your work. You may wish to keep this information separate to your work equipment.

This log is helpful for a number of reasons. In order to help you decide whether to escalate the matter or take other measures, it first clarifies the frequency and severity of the behaviour. Second, it produces a factual report that you can consult if you need to discuss the issue with HR or a supervisor. Your written records are an essential tool for building credibility and making sure that your concerns are taken seriously because of the inclination of the offenders in toxic workplaces to minimise their acts, or reject responsibility. We know that women are often branded as 'emotional' when raising complaints, so having an objective list shows that you've been thorough and methodical, which can help you make a stronger case.

Despite the main focus of documentation being practicality, this method may provide mental advantages. By putting incidents in writing, you can externalise the issue and distance yourself from the negative actions occurring around you. It confirms that the toxicity is a result of a problem in the environment or the people who are sustaining it, not a reflection of your value or skill. This act of acknowledgement gives you the capacity to transition from feeling powerless to taking proactive measures towards resolution.

Establishing clear boundaries is important. Restricting interactions and acting professionally can assist you in managing toxic people and lessen their influence on you. Toxic people frequently take advantage of your emotional reactions. Focus on managing what you can, such as your time, your reactions, and your mental space, even if this may be easier said than done. Find opportunities to cut out pointless exchanges, such as gossip, and focus your energies on doing your work as effectively as possible. Create a network of support outside of the workplace at the same time. Sharing your experiences with loved ones, friends, or dependable mentors can provide emotional support and serve as a reminder that you are not alone. In some cases, you might also find allies within the workplace who share your concerns. A sense of camaraderie with others experiencing the same struggles can help you feel less isolated, and give you a collective voice to address broader workplace issues.

Maintaining your physical and emotional health is essential while you're under constant stress. Making self-care a top priority can help you develop resilience because toxic situations can negatively impact your health. Small, regular behaviours can have a significant impact. For example, regular exercise, a good diet, and a regular sleep pattern can all help you focus better and feel less stressed. Investigate mindfulness practices to help you maintain your composure under pressure, such as meditation, or deep breathing exercises. Another effective method for managing emotions is thinking back on your experiences and processing them through journalling. This may remind you of how we've addressed burnout, but it's especially prevalent for a toxic workplace, as toxicity can be the root of burnout.

It could be time to escalate the matter if your attempts to manage the toxicity within yourself are not improving the situation. Think about discussing your issues with your HR department or a dependable manager. Frame your criticism in a positive way during these discussions, emphasising how the toxic workplace affects not only you but also the team's output, morale, and general work culture. Be ready to discuss possible solutions and provide the log that you have gathered. Recognise though, that not all workplaces are capable or willing to successfully address structural challenges. Start preparing an exit strategy if the toxicity doesn't go away. Leaving a toxic workplace can be a life-changing move towards regaining your career and well-being, despite how difficult it may appear. It could be as small as updating your CV, refining your LinkedIn profile, or expanding your professional network. When contemplating a move, research companies with strong reputations for positive workplace culture, and identify roles that align with your skills, values, and aspirations.

Finally, we encourage you to remind yourself that your value and ability are not defined by a toxic work environment. It's easy to absorb the negativity, but you have to make a conscious effort to keep your identity apart from the situation. You can give yourself the ability to take charge again and move forwards by protecting yourself, dealing with the problems in a positive way.

Time to get real- stories from the industry

It is important to recognise that 'lemons' can look and feel different to different people, and can come in all shapes and sizes. Whilst the answers we have shared so far in this chapter have been from our own understanding, we wanted to create a safe space for other individuals to anonymously share how they handled some of the challenging situations they have experienced.

Some of this next section may be triggering or upsetting, so please approach cautiously and step away if it doesn't feel right, or if you need space. Again, remember there are helplines at the front of this book and lots of organisations ready to talk and help if some of the topics discussed hit home a little too much.

We are very proud to include these experiences and thank them for their candour and openness. We share these experiences in the hope you too will resonate and take solace in the fact that you are not alone, if you too have been subject to this behaviour.

Finally, it's important to share that the individuals who share the following stories do so in their own words, with their own voice and from their own lived experiences. They have been able to overcome these challenges with support, and throw those 'manky lemons' away!

Disclaimer – The responses in this section to the questions, are the respondent's own perspectives and opinions.

Story One - 'Punished for progress'.

I find this hard to talk about because I have always tried really hard to get along with everyone, but on this occasion it just didn't happen. This story makes me feel sad, like a part of my career is tarnished. Whilst I'm happy now, this experience took a lot to get over and did see me have to lean on new management and therapists for support.

I think lots of us have it sewn into us to keep progressing and developing in our careers. With that ambition and motivation, it naturally means people will progress and develop to a point they move on and take their next career step. I'd been working in a very hectic cybersecurity business unit, and had really been prioritising my development and learning. It got to the point I could pursue a new job opportunity, and I genuinely thought my leadership would be delighted for me. I thought we had a good relationship and that they'd want to see me take that next career step. I was excited to show them that all of the awesome things they'd taught me, had turned into a fantastic next step.

Having the 'I'm leaving' chat is never easy, but I went into my scheduled meeting ready to tell them I was off. I was happy, excited and nervous. I told my leader and it just went downhill from there. Immediately, I was met with anger and disappointment. I was told I'd 'betrayed' my team, and that I had let everyone down. I was made to feel like what I was doing was selfish, and that in many ways, I'd wasted everyone's time. This shook me to my absolute core, and if I'm honest broke my heart. I cared about my leader, and to feel like he hated me was overwhelmingly upsetting and set off a lot of anxieties in me.

I tried to stay strong but every day working grew harder and harder. My leader refused to talk to me, and told others not to work with me. He removed all my access and cut me out of every meeting until I felt isolated and alone. I had a few trusted friends tell me he'd said in a team meeting that I was 'dead to him'. I can't fathom it and it very nearly broke me. I'd never been treated so horribly before.

For the remainder of my time, I just stuck my head in the sand and did what I could with the remaining accesses, friends and meetings I had. I had to accept this was a 'him' problem not a 'me' problem. In the beginning, I tried to self-justify why he was treating me this way (maybe he's unhappy, maybe there's something else going on etc), but actually, I shouldn't have. I had done nothing wrong and my career was for me to own and drive as I saw fit. He had no right to make me feel so worthless and unhappy.

I can reflect back now and say it has made me stronger and more resilient. I do probably still care too much what people think about me, but I think that's just the way I'm built. I guess I've also learnt that you can't please everyone, so please yourself! Final lesson is that I really did, and continue to, speak to the people around me for support and help. I couldn't have handled this experience alone; it was the people around me that I trusted that kept me going in such a dark moment.

Story Two - 'Will you be having more babies?'

I am lucky to have been able to have kids. I know there's lots of people who can't, and I don't want to complain or seem ungrateful. But having kids, has, on many occasions, led me to being stigmatised and treated differently. It's been when I've needed time off to care for one of them when a project is due, or just the fact that work is my second priority and they know that.

This particular situation shocked me really as in this day and age, I didn't think it was still happening. But sadly, I can testify that it is.

I was applying for a new role, having had my kids, and obviously the career gaps come with that. When I applied, during the process itself I was treated fairly and kindly. I was really excited for the role, and I'd been told I basically had it. But then when I had a catch up privately after the last interview with the hiring leader, he asked me outright 'will you be having more babies? It's just we need someone who will be here to do the role properly.' He made it feel like it was a caveat to me securing the position. It had been hard before to step out of work and halt my career, and now it felt like my choice to be a mum was almost being frowned upon and limiting my ability to have new roles and prospects.

At the time, I didn't know how to take it and the question threw me. I hadn't really thought about whether or not I wanted more kids but I knew I wanted the role. I felt I had to say 'no' to the question, and then a few days later I got the job. I can't say whether my answer swayed the decision, but to me it feels like it did.

The job itself was great, and was a stepping stone in my career, but I do always wonder 'what if'. What if I had said yes to wanting more children? What if I had become pregnant whilst I was in the role? I'm disappointed that I don't feel I was taken for my skillset and qualities, but instead that was a side product to being of childbearing age.

I'm not working for that company anymore but whilst I was there, I enjoyed the role. What I would say though, is that no-one in any position should be asking you that. First off, it's assumptive that someone wants or even can have kids. Secondly, you'd never ask a man that question. And thirdly... it's no one else's business but your own. This was a red flag and now I'm older I can see that.

Story Three- 'Office Hot'

I don't really know how to talk about this, because for a long time, I convinced myself it wasn't really happening, or at least, that it wasn't a big deal. I've always tried to be friendly at work. But this… made me feel like I was being punished for something I couldn't control. It started subtly. A comment here and there, someone saying I was 'office hot' like it was a compliment I should be grateful for. At first, I brushed it off. Maybe they were just being friendly. Maybe I was imagining it. Maybe I should just laugh along and not make a fuss. But it didn't stop there. Men I worked closely with, some of whom I had to rely on day-to-day, would get drunk at socials and see me as fair game. A hand on my thigh, and whispered comments that far crossed the line. The next day, they'd act like nothing had happened, like I should pretend it didn't either. It was always 'We were all a bit messy last night, weren't we?', as if that made it okay.

It wasn't just the nights out, though. It was the over-familiarity during the day. The comments about my outfits, things like 'You're really making it hard to focus on work today.' It made me feel like I was only there to be admired, not respected. The worst part was the guilt. I started to question myself-was I being too friendly? Was I leading them on by just existing? Was it really that bad? Other people seemed to find it funny. Maybe I should just be flattered.

But I wasn't. I was uncomfortable. I toned myself down in ways I didn't even realise until I looked back. I'd stopped wearing outfits I'd loved 'just in case' I was harassed.

I wish I could say it stopped completely, even after I raised it, I felt like the one at fault. But, I just learned how to manage it better. I leaned on colleagues I trusted. I called things out when I felt safe to do so.

I know now that I am more than how I look. More than what they say when they've had one too many.

Story Four - Drinking Culture

I'm a non-drinker for lots of reasons. It makes me feel rubbish, I don't like hangovers and it just doesn't work for me. I don't preach about it; it's just something I have chosen to do for me. What I have found hard though in my cybersecurity career, is that all client or team mate socials seem to revolve around drinking. I don't feel I am thought about when these arrangements are made and it leaves me feeling really left out.

As an example, there was this 'start of financial year kick-off' where the launch was held in a brewery. I don't mind being around alcohol or others drinking, but when I arrived at the event I was described as the 'boring one', and that I was uptight. I watched as everyone around me descended into drunken chaos and with that came a thrusted responsibility to start looking after people who had taken it too far. The language changed, the energy changed, and people became liabilities.

Now as I said, I'm fine with people drinking, go have fun, but I'm not your Mum and I'm most definitely not boring. I wasn't on the same wave-length of any of these people, and actually I just felt really different and really lonely.

There isn't much to take from this story, but just that it's ok to not be like anyone else. Don't be peer pressured into doing things that don't feel right for you. These days, I don't work in this department so it's not such a problem, but I do steer clear of drinking related activities or socials, especially when I know that I will be expected to clean up the mess afterwards!

And maybe a sneaky addition (even though I said I was done)…it is not flattering to be asked by a drunk professional who you don't know 'who's this beautiful lady?'…a story for another time!

Story Five - 'You arrange the card and flowers'

I wanted to share this just to show that challenges don't have to be massive, they can just be annoying. One thing that really irritates me, is that my gender and other people's biases, means I often get lumbered with tasks that I shouldn't be. I am senior in cybersecurity, I work just as hard (if not harder) than others, but I still end up doing things simply because they are associated with typical gender roles.

There are loads of examples but I'll share this one that happened last week. A person in my office is leaving and so we are all obviously sad, but want to give them a good send off. I am in a meeting room with my all-male team and immediately one of them says 'X, you arrange the cards and flowers?' I'm not beneath the task, but when I questioned why me, I was told because 'women know about flowers and stuff'.

Now I am a confident woman and can hold my own, but this just threw me. Because I am a woman, and in fact the only woman in my team, I can do the flowers because my gender identity says I know about it best! Wow. This is just an example, and it happens all the time. It's making tea for partner business meetings; it's being the minute taker always; it's being the one to order lunches. I know I should say no but I also am worried about sticking my head above the parapet and being viewed as difficult.

I took from this that bias, unconscious or not, is real, and those around us should be doing better to squash it. I need to be brave enough to question it and push back, and I hope with time I'll get there.

And that's only a few!

Reading these stories, it's clear that challenges come in many different forms-some blatant, others subtle, but all capable of leaving a nasty impact. Whilst it's easy for us to be positive and uplifting in this book, these experiences highlight the real struggles many face in the workplace and beyond.

But what stands out just as strongly, is the resilience of the women in each of these stories. These women refused to let their experiences define them, and instead, they found ways to push forward and reclaim their space.

If any of these stories resonate with you, please know that you are not alone. It's okay to feel frustrated, hurt, or even unsure about how to respond in the moment. What matters is that you are eventually able to advocate for the respect and recognition you deserve. And for those reading who haven't faced these particular challenges, we encourage you to listen to those who have, and support if you are able to.

So, whether your 'lemon' is a bad boss, outdated biases, or a toxic culture, remember: you have the power to throw it away. And if you need help, there are always people, resources, and support systems ready to back you.

Now, let's move forward-one less 'manky lemon' at a time.

Chapter 7- Closing Words

Another chapter, leaving us all with an awful lot to think about. Life, and in particular careers, are not always sunshine and roses. We have to be accountable to our needs, beliefs, and well-being, and turn lemons into lemonade whenever we can. We need to use our knowledge and skills, and proactively turn negative experiences on their heads. We don't deserve to feel rubbish, and most importantly, we don't deserve to be unseen or unheard.

It is also worth adding to this conclusion, that there is lots of support out there for identifying roles, volunteering opportunities and even CV workshops. If you're based in the UK, remember there are institutions like the JobCentre and Citizen's Advice, that would be delighted to help you should you want to spend time working on some of these topics with an actual person.

An important message to end on. A lot of what we have spoken to in this section, relies on personal advocation and resiliency. This isn't always easy to come by, so when the 'lemons' are rife, leverage your support network, allies and advocates to help you summon your inner strength. You do not have to face challenges alone. As well, good or bad, you may find others in your community going through very similar issues, that you can then fight together.

8 GALS GO GHOSTBUSTING (THOSE PESKY MYTHS)

Entering and thriving in male-dominated fields, such as cybersecurity, comes with a unique blend of opportunities and challenges. For many of us, the path is influenced by both personal goals and outside opinions (a lot of them). However, that well-intentioned advice we receive might come out as conflicting or even out of date. How do we cut through these myths and find the realities of what it takes to be successful, develop, and flourish in such a setting? That's where we come in!

We'll dissect some of these myths and misconceptions in this chapter, peeling back the layers to examine what is real, what is overblown, and what merits actual thought. The way that societal conventions influence how we view careers, the expectations that are placed on women in fields that are dominated by men, and the very personal choices we make about how to live our professional lives, are all examples of things that are more than just facts. In an environment where the rules aren't always obvious, we'll work together to help you to question outdated beliefs, and investigate strategies to forge a genuine and sustainable path.

I am so conflicted. I am told to have a career and make money, but I'm also expected to do all the chores, childcare, manage the running of our family home, be happy and healthy and a role model AHHHHHH. Is this normal? I'm exhausted!

Ah the joy of gender roles in the modern world! This question feels like a part of the speech in the Barbie film by America Ferrera:

'You have to be thin, but not too thin. And you can never say you want to be thin. You have to say you want to be healthy, but also you have to be thin. You have to have money, but you can't ask for money because that's crass. You have to be a boss, but you can't be mean. You have to lead, but you can't squash other people's ideas. You're supposed to love being a mother, but don't talk about your kids all the damn time. You have to be a career woman but also always be looking out for other people.'

More than ever, women are juggling. This is not to diminish the efforts of any other person or gender, but there is something to be said for the sheer volume of women that we alone speak to, that feel they are sinking further and further under the weight of their tasks, jobs and responsibilities. To be doing so much you feel like you're almost drowning is not normal at all....

But unfortunately, it has become normalised... and that's the problem.

You should not have to do it all, but the pressure to do it is real. This is often driven by the urge to make it all happen, through an unwillingness to say no or ask for help, and sadly more often than not, just because it's expected of us and we don't feel empowered to challenge or change that.

Now, neither of us can preach too loudly as we both are very guilty of taking on too much, and subsequently wearing ourselves out. But we can share some tactics we've employed that have helped lighten the load and the pressure.

- **Get help with the house**- we wish we could employ every reader a fabulous cleaner or home help, but that just isn't feasible! But what we can recommend is to leverage what you have around you. Whether it's housemates, kids or a partner, create a chores list and hold folks accountable to what they need to be doing. Split it fairly and equally, but with flex space in case something comes up that means a particular chore cannot be accomplished in a singular day. Take time to get organised and sort out that cupboard under the sink, so when it does come to chores, what you need is ready to go. Everyone should be pulling their weight. And if you do have the accessibility of a cleaner, there is no shame in having that support, if it helps you to lighten the load.

- **Talk it through**-if you are feeling overwhelmed, talk to your support network. Maybe those around you just don't realise that you're struggling! By sharing with your partner or friends how you're feeling, you will likely find people offer support or to take some of the 'load'. As an example, if you're struggling to finish work and do the pick-ups, talking to a school Mum friend may mean you can share the responsibilities and form a 'pick up crew' which means twice a week you have an extra half hour at home! Every second counts when time is stretched, but if you don't ask or share, you don't get. Talk to someone you can trust.
- **Assess the tasks at hand**- do you have to be the one to do the task? Could someone else help? Are you being too controlling of the task? Can you say no? Again, a lot of women in particular feel pressurised into taking on all the responsibilities or tasks at hand. There's a multitude of reasons as to why, but we promise it doesn't have to always be you that does it all. You can switch it up and say no, or even 'I can't do it now but I can do it on X date'. Another tip when it comes to work taskings, is to share when you can't do something and delegate the competing tasks or responsibilities you have. You then empower your leader and directly ask them to prioritise the list and tell you what should wait. This in itself can be a huge eye opener to how much you're doing and the sustainability of that! Look at everything you're doing, and really dig into whether it must be done by you, and whether it must be done right now.
- **Schedule in 'me time'**-tasks can feel too much when we haven't taken the time to recalibrate and make time for self-care. Intentionally schedule into your work calendar, breaks, lunch, and if you can, time to exercise, so you know you can meet your needs. Another idea may be to find a pre-scheduled exercise class that happens the same time every week, so you can build that into yours and your family's routines. Prioritise you for once! It will help.

Ultimately, we all need to take a long hard look and accept we simply cannot do it all. It is impossible. We can try, and push, and beat ourselves up, but it won't change the fact if you feel you're doing too much, you most likely are. A mantra we have repeated a lot in this book – but please be kind to yourself. If one day you are just too exhausted, it is fine to be happy with just doing enough to get by. If you have to say no to a piece of work or a school friend's party, if you have to cancel plans because you're knackered, it's okay. The folks that love you and care about you, will understand. Focus on doing you, and not always doing everything for everyone else.

I am told to bring my authentic self to work, but should I really?

In writing this book, we've discussed the idea of authenticity, a lot. Likely more than we had done in our lifetimes prior to writing this book. We want to be honest with you, as readers, but is the fear of judgement, or the ugly truth perhaps a bit off-putting if you were to share all of you? Yes.

The idea of bringing your authentic self to work is both deeply appealing, and inherently nuanced. In theory, being authentic at work means showing up as your true self, sharing the true versions of your thoughts, values, personality, and even vulnerabilities. It's about aligning who you are on the inside with how you present yourself externally. But in practice, this ideal often collides with workplace realities, creating a tension between authenticity and professionalism that is not always easy to navigate.

In order to provide a more thorough response, we need to think about what it means to be authentic in a work environment. Being authentic doesn't always include oversharing every part of who you are, or ignoring the standards set by your employer. Rather, it's about being truthful and loyal to your basic values whilst also being aware of your surroundings and the people in them.

Our level of authenticity at work is greatly influenced by our fear of how we are perceived. If our genuine selves don't fit with workplace standards or expectations, many of us fear judgement, misunderstanding, or even punishment. Self-censorship, in which we modify our words and behaviours to conform to social norms, is the output of this. It's adaptation, not necessarily inauthentic. Because people are social creatures, relationships and reputations are important in the job. It can occasionally backfire to be too 'authentic', in a way that ignores these dynamics, resulting in unforeseen consequences like strained relationships.

It's also very important to understand that authenticity is a spectrum, rather than a binary state. There is a middle ground; you don't have to be totally guarded or totally genuine. If you were to rate your level of 'authenticity' on a scale of 1 to 100 on a normal weekday, most of us would probably score lower than 70. This just represents the organic adaptations we make to function in our work contexts; it doesn't suggest that we are dishonest or deceptive. It all comes down to deciding which aspects of ourselves we would rather keep private and which we feel secure enough to share.

The culture of the company also has a big impact on how you bring your true self to work. Certain organisations intentionally promote authenticity by appreciating uniqueness and a range of viewpoints. Full sincerity may appear uncomfortable or unfeasible to others due to strict rules or implicit expectations. You could find it simpler to be real if your place of employment promotes a psychologically secure environment where individuals feel appreciated, respected, and free to express themselves without worrying about the repercussions. On the other hand, you may feel pressured to suppress aspects of yourself in settings that encourage conformity or penalise diversity.

The idea of boundaries, which we've explored plenty of times before in this book, is an additional layer to take into account. Sharing every detail about ourselves is not a need for authenticity. Professionalism and emotional health depend on having healthy boundaries. You may decide to keep your personal hardships or thoughts on delicate subjects' private while being transparent about your beliefs, work style, or interests. You can respect the dynamics of the job while remaining true to yourself.

Ultimately, how you define authenticity, what you feel comfortable revealing, and how it fits with your career objectives will determine whether or not you should bring your true self to work. You don't have to give everyone access to your inner life, and it's totally fine to modify how you present yourself depending on the situation. Being true to who you are at work is not a binary choice. It means striking a balance between staying loyal to your basic beliefs, and making adjustments for the demands of your workplace. Finding an authentic version of yourself that respects your limits, feels real to you, and fits in with your working culture is crucial.

Can we really have it all, as women in a male dominated industry?

It makes us angry that this is a narrative that exists. Because in short...nobody can have it all. If we can tell you one lesson, above anything, it is that you cannot, and we repeat, cannot be everything, to everyone, all of the time. Yet as women, we're expected to, and expect ourselves, to 'have it all'.

Rant over.

Let's examine this further though, as the issue of 'having it all', in a male-dominated field involves more than just juggling work and personal obligations; it also involves the deeply rooted expectations and structural injustices that disproportionately affect women. The idea of 'having it all' is essentially faulty. It portrays an ideal existence in which you may succeed professionally, create a fulfilling personal life, uphold solid bonds with others, be there for your loved ones, and manage to find time for your own health. Let's face it: no one, regardless of gender, can achieve this ideal. However, the pressure to succeed is considerably greater for women, particularly in fields where men make up the majority of the population.

This notion of 'having it all' indicates that women should be able to smoothly balance every position society demands of them, dedicated professional, loving partner, committed parent or guardian (if that's what you'd like), supportive friend, all while preserving an impression of effortless composure. And it's simple to feel as though we've failed not only ourselves, but also those who rely on us when we unavoidably fail. We know, and you know, it's SO hard. This is especially insufferable since it ignores the structural obstacles that hinder women's success in environments where men predominate. The larger structural problems, such as unequal compensation, restricted access to leadership positions, a lack of flexibility, and prejudices that diminish women's contributions, are more important than individual effort.

These challenges are undoubtedly exacerbated in male-dominated fields by the requirement to continuously demonstrate your legitimacy and value. Why is the bar so much higher for us? In order to be regarded as equals, women frequently experience pressure to put in more effort, be more intelligent, and accomplish more than their masculine counterparts. We are frequently expected to behave or lead in a traditionally masculine manner while also facing criticism for not being 'feminine enough. Ever been told you're too 'bossy?' This becomes an exhausting cycle of self-monitoring and adaptation that just perpetuates the pressure of the already unachievable goal of 'having it all. Eye roll...

In actuality, aiming for this unreachable standard might be very costly-

mentally. When the thought of 'having it all' doesn't match reality, it frequently results in feelings of inadequacy, dissatisfaction, and fatigue. It's also important for us to stress that women are not to blame for this. Workplace arrangements and social conventions that continue to place disproportionate demands on women without offering the required support networks are to blame. Requiring women to 'have it all', is nothing more than setting them up for failure in the absence of structural improvements, such as fair compensation, complete parental leave laws, reasonably priced childcare, mentorship programs, and job flexibility.

And this may good be a good point to ask yourself 'has my male colleague ever been asked if he can have it all?'...

What is the other option, then? Rather than chasing the illusion of 'having it all', it's important to redefine what personal fulfilment and achievement really mean. For you, what does having enough mean? What is the most important thing in your life? By asking yourself these questions, you can develop a vision of success that is not influenced by social norms, but rather fits with your beliefs, objectives, and general well-being. It involves learning to set priorities, letting go of perfectionism, learning to say no, and concentrating on the things that make you happy and give you meaning.

So, we've relieved ourselves of the continual pressure to perform above expectations, we now also have to establish a precedent for redefining success for women in these fields by changing the emphasis from an impossible ideal to one that is both realistic and individual. This is about confronting the seriously faulty narratives that have been spread for far too long, not about letting go of goals or settling for less. This change is about more than just personal preferences in the larger scheme of things. But this also involves advocating for structural change. Women are not only responsible for the weight of 'having it all'; everyone bears some of the obligation. This entails reconsidering workplace regulations, tackling prejudices, and cultivating environments where women are not only accepted, but assisted in accomplishing their objectives without being held to impossible standards.

'Having it all' is ultimately a myth, and a harmful one at that. It's acceptable for no one to constantly be everything to everyone. Instead, we may concentrate on establishing boundaries, figuring out what really matters, and creating a life that feels purposeful and happy for us. By doing this, we move closer to embracing a more genuine and sustainable future, and rejecting the irrational expectations society has set on us. Success in a male-dominated field, or any other, should never be equated with 'having it all.'

It should be about having enough and realising that you are already enough just the way you are.

I have it drilled into me to keep progressing and developing. Is it ok to just stay where I am?

Between the consistent end of year reviews and goal planning, the pings for promotions on LinkedIn, and the flurry of courses, events, and community groups, it can feel like the buzz of progress and development is everywhere. Whilst for some people this fits their needs and career plans, for others it is the wrong time or just of no interest whatsoever. If you are happy, life is moving as you like it, and the stars are aligned, there is nothing wrong with enjoying your role for exactly what it is and where you are. There is something genuinely beautiful about being able to enjoy the moment you're in and be satisfied with the cards you have at hand.

This can sometimes go against workplace culture, where we have it drilled into us that we must keep striving for more, and taking on more responsibilities. But again, if you are satisfied and fulfilled, own that! Be clear on how you feel with your leadership, and show your contentment in the work you produce. There is no rule you must climb the ranks, or take on new positions. Your career is your destiny to control.

There isn't really a lot more to say in response to this question! We just want you to be happy! So, to end we just want to say, be sure not to close yourself down to progress and development. Yes, you can be enjoying life for what it's offering, but you never quite know when an interesting opportunity may pass your desk. Continue to be engaged in your community and be open to ideas others share with you. Whilst you may not want it right now, it may be worth exploring again in the future.

How can I deal with imposter syndrome when I am one of the few women in my field?

Imposter syndrome is one of those 'nasties' that impacts individuals regardless of their gender, but, it does appear to disproportionately impact us as women.

According to VeryWell Mind, 'imposter syndrome is the feeling of being a fraud or phony despite your achievements or skills'. Relatable, right? As a woman in a male-dominated field, these feeling of self-doubt, feelings of being an actual imposter, can rear their ugly head regardless of whether it's even true, and regardless of your accomplishments or skillsets. These feelings can then filter beyond the boundaries of work, and go on to impact your home life, relationships, and day-to-day activities. The insecurities can feel very real, and very consuming, which is why you must face them head on.

Before we share some ideas for overcoming and managing imposter syndrome, we wanted to share some findings from research Dr. Valerie Young (writer and founder of the Imposter Syndrome Institute). Her research identified five types of imposter syndrome. Which one resonates with you?

- The Perfectionist-this type of imposter syndrome revolves around the belief that anything less than absolute perfection, means you could have performed better and may have even failed. This individual often beats themselves up and holds themselves to a very high standard.
- The Expert-this person feels like an imposter because they don't possess complete knowledge about a subject, a process or maintain subject-matter expertise. The constant awareness of 'more to learn', they never feel they fit with an 'expert' title. They never feel as 'good' as someone else and can question what they bring to their team or to a conversation.
- The Natural Genius-if something isn't mastered quickly or doesn't come naturally, you question your legitimacy. This type of person feels like an imposter because they believe they don't have a natural gift and/or level of intelligence.
- The Soloist-this type of imposter syndrome is born off the back of having to ask for help to get something done. The Soloist doubts their capabilities and competencies because they couldn't accomplish something on their own.
- The Superperson-this really fits with the 'always saying yes' person we have spoken about before. This individual truly believes they must work harder, faster, longer, and hold themselves to often impossibly high levels of personal accomplishment. If then they can't keep up or something goes wrong, they feel like they are a failure.

Whilst we don't always have to feel imposter syndrome all the time, the majority of mentees we have spoken to (and even us as writers) have experienced at least one of these imposter syndrome types at least once in their lives. And whilst it may appear once in a blue moon, when it does it can be upsetting, demoralising, fear-inducing, and even disappointing.

The original question posed, connected imposter syndrome and being 'the only woman in your field'. Imposter syndrome can go hand in hand with the fact you may be different to your peers, you may come from a different background, community, or gender to the rest of the team around you, and that can make you feel all the 'imposter' feelings life can throw at you. We validate that and we see you. How can you get past it?

First off, you need to talk it out. This is becoming a reoccurring theme, but when you're dealing with imposter syndrome. Talking to a trusted person can help. Dig in to how you are feeling, its legitimacy, and even why you believe you feel that way. Dissect, analyse, and talk through the situation and work with your trusted person to understand what you need to make it easier to handle and manage. You need to question the thoughts and the intrusiveness of them to your role and your life. Is what you're saying real, or are you just being plain old cruel to yourself? Does the imposter syndrome have any base, at all?

When you have imposter syndrome, a behaviour you need to embrace is to stop comparing yourself to everyone else. Life would be incredibly boring if we were all the same, so why are you comparing yourself so intensely and relentlessly to Debbie, Dave or Denise? You don't have to be the same. The reason you are in your team and organisation is because you bring something to the conversation and to the success of the practice and effort. By constantly comparing yourself, you will, of course, find differences, because you fundamentally aren't them! Take some time to list what you bring to the table, and own that. You are unique, and that is fantastic.

Now, say there is a gap or a skill that someone else is better at. First off, that's fine! That's why, as humans, we grow and evolve. If it is a skill or attribute that you actually need or want to have, you can build it into your development plan. As an example, say that Denise is amazing at Excel and every time you use it, you feel anxious and overstimulated. Why not chat to Denise and see if she can help squash some of those feelings by teaching you, or pointing you in the direction of resources to learn? Don't let imposter syndrome limit you, and instead acknowledge it, and where possible come up with a proactive plan to overcome whatever it is that is making you feel the way you are.

Another powerful way to manage imposter syndrome is to reframe your mindset and actively acknowledge your achievements… the return of the 'smug list'. Our brains are wired to focus on negative thoughts more than positive ones, which means we often dwell on what we think we lack rather than what we have accomplished. This could be as simple as a physical notebook, a digital document, or even a folder in your email where you save praise from colleagues or clients. Reviewing this regularly, especially during moments of doubt, can serve as a tangible reminder that your success is not a fluke, but a result of your hard work.

Another key strategy is to reframe failure as part of growth. Those who struggle with imposter syndrome often see mistakes as proof that they don't belong, rather than as natural learning opportunities. Instead of allowing one setback to confirm your doubts, challenge yourself to adopt a growth mindset. When negative thoughts arise, ask yourself: 'what would I say to a friend in this situation?' You likely wouldn't tell them they don't belong or that they aren't good enough, so why treat yourself that way? Practicing self-compassion and speaking to yourself with the same kindness and encouragement you would offer a close friend can help shift your perspective.

If you've suffered with imposter syndrome, you will know that it comes with a lot of beating yourself up. We promise you that no-one is perfect. No-one can do everything. No-one can accomplish everything alone. As we have said already, everyone brings a piece of themselves to their industry. That could be skills, experiences, thought leadership, and personal qualities. It's a combination of unique skills and experience that we can use to accomplish incredible things. And you are one of those unique people.

So, to end with this final message. If you're feeling of being an imposter is driven by you being a woman and maybe a 'rare species' in your workplace, please know there are other women out there feeling the exact same way. It's a horrible feeling when you look around a metaphorical room and see no one that looks or feels like you. This is why employee resource groups and community groups are so critical. If we relate this specifically to cybersecurity, there are many women in industry working in cybersecurity roles across different organisations-but these women are drastically outnumbered and poorly represented in comparison to their male counterpart. This is the cybersecurity gender gap we hear spoken about so much, and why so many diversity, equity and inclusion initiatives are underway in the sector.

If you are feeling alone or imposter syndrome is eating away, a sure-fire way to target that is through finding others like 'you'. To help with this effort, here are some 'Women in Cyber' styled groups that you look at in this book appendices, and connect with to find new friends, allies and like-minded people:

- Women in Cybersecurity (WiCyS)
- Hacker in Heels
- LMF Network (Like Minded Females)
- Women + cybersecuritysecurity - Women's Society of Cyberjutsu
- Women of FIRST
- Motherboard
- Halzak/Elevate

Don't be alone! There are so many people out there who will be happy to hear you and support you.

Chapter 8-Closing Words

Although the myths and misconceptions surrounding jobs in male-dominated fields might occasionally feel like roadblocks, they also offer chances for development and reinterpretation. We can start to see these tall tales for what they are, often partial truths influenced by outmoded conventions, conventional viewpoints, or over generalised guidance…by challenging them. The truth is much messier and, in many respects, liberating.

A clearer, personalised plan for navigating fields that are overwhelmingly male becomes apparent as we debunk these myths. The secret is not just to question the accepted status quo, but also to make room for your own definition of success, one that takes into account your particular objectives, goals, and abilities. By doing this, you're not only giving yourself more power, but you're also helping to change how we view and assist women in these fields more broadly. The myths may endure, but they don't have to dictate your course if you have clarity, self-assurance, and a sense of community.

9 SETTING THE SCENE FOR YOU TO THRIVE

Embarking on a fruitful career, particularly as a woman in a predominantly male industry, requires not just knowledge and skills, but a strategic approach to making the 'magic' happen. We need to be bringing everything we have learnt and experienced together, to create a positive scene for success. That can be anything from lessons learned to 'smugs' and 'joys', to brand and associated behaviours. When these are aligned, you have the power to absolutely smash it!

Our goal is to empower you with the tools, knowledge, and mindset necessary to not merely survive, but truly thrive in the field of cybersecurity. We want you to find happiness and fulfilment in what you do, within your own boundaries and in the way you decide. We will help you set the foundations to really allow yourself to do that.

As I'm trying to grow in my career, how can I find ways to free up more time for meaningful work?

There is an unspoken rule, that within the first few years of any career, you must accept every opportunity, be it within work or outside, and that's the strategy to grow. Fast forward five years, from our own experiences, often this can lead to a packed diary, a mountain of commitments, and a whole lot of guilt. We're not encouraging you to be limited in what you accept, however, if you feel that you're burdened with a lifestyle of doing work for others, as opposed to work that meaningfully impacts you and your own growth, you may want to consider freeing up some of that time for the work that makes an impact on your career. We want to give you the means to match your everyday tasks with your long-term career objectives.

Most importantly, and perhaps an area in which we can't support you in, is defining what 'meaningful' actually means. Meaningful may mean actively working towards a promotion, but it could also mean working towards a better work and life balance, or for a pivot into an area of more interest. Our other chapters should help you in defining these goals, but it is ultimately down to you.

Once you've defined what the end-goal is, you can start to put some practical strategies in place to achieve this. It's key to review and improve any task prioritisation techniques that you're currently using to further free up time for meaningful work. By doing this, you make sure that your daily tasks not only maintain your productivity, but also make a substantial contribution to your long-term objectives. You might wish to use techniques like the Eisenhower Matrix (look it up, it's fab). This concept divides tasks into four quadrants based on their importance and urgency: important but not urgent tasks that are essential for long-term success, urgent but not important tasks that could be delegated, urgent and important tasks that need immediate attention, and tasks that are neither important nor urgent and can be completely eliminated. You can concentrate your efforts by making a list of all your tasks, and honestly allocating each to the relevant quadrant.

Efficient work management needs regular evaluation. Weekly review sessions offer a way to evaluate what has been done, and what needs improvement. You can assess both finished and unfinished work during this time, reorder your priorities in light of new obligations, and make sure your actions support your long-term objectives. You may also wish to plan more in-depth monthly or quarterly sessions, in addition to weekly evaluations. These in-depth evaluations provide an opportunity to revisit long-term goals, spot patterns in your to-do list, and modify your approach accordingly.

Similarly, working on your time management and scheduling techniques is another effective tactic. Adopt time blocking by allocating some periods of your day to concentrated tasks that work towards your goals. For example, if you are given study time within your working week, and studying towards a specific certification is meaningful to advancing your career, blocking that time clearly in your calendar can mean that you aren't cramming it into an already-rammed schedule. Set clear limits with coworkers and turn off alerts to reduce disruptions during these blocks (we love the Teams DND feature!). But word of warning... It is then with you, and you alone to hold yourself accountable to using this time for 'meaningful' activities, and not just have a nap, or get distracted!

If not having the time for the tasks you want to complete is the issue, we can also recommend automation and delegation. Looking at your daily schedule to find any tasks that could be streamlined with technology or assigned to team members may give you some time back to focus on more meaningful work. Your workload can be greatly decreased by automating repetitive operations, whether with workflow automation software, email filters, or even by hiring virtual help (although we recognise that this comes from great privilege). If you are going to delegate to others, it's crucial to make sure that when you assign, you properly explain expectations and give your colleagues the help they need to succeed. Use a tracker to keep note of what was on your plate, what you have shared out, and what you're waiting on. You can then keep on top of the spinning plates and have a true accurate list of what you're working towards.

Lastly, concentrate on developing an attitude that encourages continuous improvements to your productivity. Don't be scared to create limits to safeguard your time, and learn to say no to requests that don't fit with your priorities…more on this later in the chapter. You might also consider seeking feedback from mentors or peers who may offer new perspectives on managing your workload and working towards your goals. As we have already said -we can give you all these fabulous tips, but it's on you to be accountable and make the magic happen. If you want it, go get it, and make sure you have the time and space to smash it to the best of your ability.

What small changes could make a big difference in my productivity or well-being?

We often believe that transformations require grand changes-an entirely new routine, a completely new set of habits, or a drastic shift in mindset. But what if the biggest improvements in productivity and well-being actually come from small, intentional changes? What if a slight tweak in our daily habits, environment, or mindset could set off a ripple effect that makes a big difference in your productivity or well-being?

By the end of this answer, we hope to show you how small, purposeful tweaks can gave you more energy, greater efficiency, and a closer sense of what your well-being actually needs. Whether you're looking for ways to reduce stress, increase focus, or just make your days feel a little lighter, the insights here will help you make progress, without the overwhelm of a complete life change.

We all think about rest as a key way to improve our well-being, but how many of us are actually organised about using our leave, and how often does it get rolled over? Using your annual leave and planning it in advance can have a profound impact on both your productivity and well-being. We, as many other people do, fall into the trap of postponing time off, waiting for the quieter moments, or fearing that stepping away will disrupt the balancing act. However, we know that research shows that regular breaks, especially time out of our 'normal' environment, significantly reduces stress, prevents burnout, and boosts longer-term focus.

When you schedule your leave in advance, you create something to look forward to, which can improve motivation during stressful periods. Planning ahead allows you to wrap up key tasks, delegate responsibilities, and return to work with a refreshed mind, rather than feeling overwhelmed by unfinished business. If you aren't in a position to use your time off, a small shift we encourage you to make is to reconsider your mindset towards annual leave. Rather than seeing time off as a luxury, you should see it as an investment into yourself. Having time away gives you the space to restore your energy to become more efficient, and importantly, recharged in your mindset.

Specifically considering productivity, taking some time to consider what works best for you in terms of your working style, is a small but mighty change that will ease the day-to-day. Whether you use digital productivity tools, paper notes, or a hybrid method, figuring out what works for you can have a big impact on how well you manage your time and concentration. There is no one-size-fits-all definition of productivity; what is extremely effective for one of us may be utterly ineffective for the other. Instead of forcing yourself to adopt a system that doesn't fit your natural workflow, the idea is to try out several approaches and see which ones actually help you stay organised.

For some, the experience of writing things down on paper by using planners or sticky notes enhances memory retention and provides a satisfying sense of accomplishment when crossing off completed tasks. Others may prefer digital tools like task managers, calendar apps, or note-taking software, such as Remarkable, that offer features such as reminders, cloud syncing, and integration with other platforms. A hybrid approach, where digital tools keep long-term plans structured while physical notes capture daily priorities, may work best for those who need both flexibility and structure. The ultimate objective is to simplify decision-making, clear out brain clutter, and develop a method that seems natural. The correct tools should increase your output without adding to your workload. Alongside achieving more, you'll feel more in control of your workflow, which we believe contributes to experiencing less stress when you take the time to identify and improve the strategy that suits you the best.

Finding the productivity strategy that works best for you is closely related to having the right office or work environment set up. Similar to how the correct tools can improve your productivity, your physical environment has a significant impact on how motivated you are, how focused you are, and how you feel overall. While a purposeful, well-organised workstation can improve focus, creativity, and even mood, a disorganised, uncomfortable, or uninspired workspace can quietly sap your energy and raise stress levels. The type of work you do and your personal preferences will determine your ideal arrangement.

While some people do best in environments that are simple and devoid of distractions, others are more focused when there are motivating quotes, plants, or background music present. Additionally, ergonomics are important. Proper desk height, comfortable seating, and sufficient lighting can all help you focus for longer amounts of time, by reducing physical strain that causes us to feel tired and demotivated. We can't all have the luxury of an office separate from our home, but we can control how we feel about the environment around us.

Even though it might seem contradictory, doing things unrelated to your job, can improve your productivity and in turn, well-being. Hobbies offer a mental reset that lets you escape the stresses of everyday life and come back with new vitality. Whether it is a skill-based hobby, like cooking, or a physical activity like hiking, yoga, or a creative endeavour like writing, these pursuits provide a sense of fulfilment that goes beyond accomplishments at work. Different brain regions are stimulated by hobbies, which promote mindfulness. As we mentioned earlier, they help you avoid burnout by providing a means to release tension, and relax without feeling bad about 'wasting time'.

And finally, and perhaps the one we've battled with the most- setting clear boundaries with technology is essential for maintaining a healthy work-life balance and sustaining long-term productivity. Work can easily intrude into personal time due to the constant availability of emails, notifications, and digital diversions, leaving little time for genuine relaxation. The brain stays in a low-level stress state without deliberate cut-off points, which makes it more difficult to completely unplug and be present in other areas of life. A much-needed separation between business and personal time can be achieved by setting a 'tech cut-off' time, which could be anything from putting your laptop away after a specific time to turning off notifications or avoiding using your phone in the bedroom. The benefits are endless- we know that you sleep better when away from screens, and having time away can help you socially.

When we are ruled by our technology, we're often more highly strung, and we all know what that causes in the home. Instead of always operating on empty, taking time away means you'll probably return to work feeling more productive, if you give your brain time to relax. The idea that productivity is about being mindful with your energy rather than being 'on' all the time is further reinforced by these time limits. You can teach yourself that sleep is equally as important as work by learning to log off at a specific time. This eventually lessens burnout, and can enhance concentration during working hours, leaving you more satisfied in both work and personal life.

How can I avoid the cost of saying 'yes' to things that don't serve me? How could I even spot that?

Avoiding the cost of saying 'yes' to things that don't serve you, involves a mixture of self-awareness, strategic decision-making, and assertiveness. For women in a field where you may already face unique challenges, including gender bias and underrepresentation, it's especially important to cultivate these skills. We know this, because we've experienced it, and so we've pulled together some tips to help you spot and avoid committing to tasks or responsibilities that don't serve your personal or professional growth:

Define Your Goals and Values:
Start by clearly defining what you want to achieve in your career and what values are important to you. This clarity will help you evaluate opportunities and requests, based on how well they align with your goals. You can read more on goal setting in Chapter 4.

Learn to Spot Time-Consuming Tasks with Low Return:
In cybersecurity, tasks that can be overly time-consuming without offering much return or growth opportunity can include excessive administrative duties, or involvement in projects that don't match your career focus. Assess how every request impacts your core work and professional development. Don't be afraid to call these out, and deprioritise them in comparison to other tasks or assignments, which not only support your organisation, but make you feel good!

Set boundaries:
Be clear about what you can and cannot take on. Setting boundaries is crucial in maintaining a focus on tasks that are beneficial to your career goals. This might mean saying no to additional responsibilities that do not contribute to your professional growth, or are outside your job scope. If you can, share these with your leadership and within your personal development or career planning. If you don't advocate for your boundaries, who will?

Harness your assertiveness:
Practice assertive communication to express your needs and rejections clearly and respectfully. This is particularly important in environments where you may be one of the few women and might feel pressured to prove your worth by taking on more than is necessary. It is a skill which can take time to get comfortable with, but practice does make perfect. We recommend finding a trusted person, and practicing with them, especially before calls or experiences where you know you will have to show assertiveness.

Seek feedback and mentorship:

Feedback from trusted colleagues and mentors can help you see if you are spending time on tasks that are beneficial. Mentors who are familiar with the dynamics of cybersecurity, can provide invaluable insights and guidance, and be able to relate this to career steps and goals.

Prioritise tasks that lead to visibility and advancement:

Focus on tasks that increase your visibility within the organisation and the broader cybersecurity community. Tasks that allow you to showcase your skills, such as leading projects, speaking at conferences, or contributing to high-profile assignments, often serve you and your career better. Additionally, if there are tasks which will not only give you the exposure, but also the lived experience to contribute towards your next career step...grab these chances! Document these kinds of taskings as you do them, get them in your 'smug' list, and be prepared to use them to demonstrate your worth and capabilities. Use them to show how you shine!

Use Time Management Tools:

Utilise tools and methods to manage your time effectively, such as prioritisation matrices or apps, such as the one we've suggested in Chapter 8, that help track how you spend your time. This can provide concrete data on whether an activity is truly worth your effort, and allow you to provide tangible metrics on how much time you are using on different elements of your role and taskings to your leadership. It is also incredibly helpful when you are trying to quantify time wasted to those who control what you do and how you do it. Being able to demonstrate this in time and then money, could not only help in the reassignment of tasks, but even support in budget requests for new technology and training.

Recognise the Signs of Overcommitment:

We won't hide that we have been individuals who have overcommitted. It is important to be aware of signs that you're taking on too much. Are you feeling constant stress? Has the quality of your work diminished? Are you not getting that all important 'job satisfaction'? These can all indicate that it's time to reassess your commitments.

By integrating these strategies into your professional life, you can more readily recognise and decline requests that do not contribute positively to your career, thereby avoiding unnecessary costs to your productivity, well-being, and professional advancement in the field of cybersecurity. Remember, every 'yes' should serve a strategic purpose in advancing your career objectives.

How can I bring others up within the industry and work towards more inclusivity?

If we want diversity and representation in our cybersecurity workforces, we need to be doing so much more. We are all accountable and responsible for supporting equality, equity, diversity, and inclusion in not only our organisations, but in the way we as individuals perform, behave, design, and empower. One of the saddest and loneliest parts of our cybersecurity careers have been the moments we have looked around and have seen no-one like us - this is what absolutely puts folks off the sector, but also discourages them for applying and progressing in the field itself. This is now one of the core reasons we now put ourselves out there - we view it as part of our duty and responsibility, to give back and bring others along for the journey. We don't want anyone to feel lonely, or like they don't belong.

When we consider this idea of 'bringing others along' and helping them achieve a seat at the metaphorical table, it really does involve a multifaceted approach. Some of it we can influence, some we can't, but if we see the bigger picture, we can really dig into the areas we can influence and change and proactively work in that space. The strategy (as we see it) spans across the areas of diversity, education, and engagement. So, let's dive in!

Diversity in hiring:

If you are in a management or hiring role, this is an element that needs significant work. We need to be looking at our team compositions. Are the teams that you are responsible for composed of individuals that come from varied backgrounds, skills, experiences, and perspectives? Hiring practices have a lot to answer for including unconscious bias in role advertising and the platforms they are shared on. The language in which we use to advertise roles, especially in cybersecurity, often deter women. A basic Google search of inclusive terminology will give you enough inspiration to sink a small ship! If you want a diverse, balanced, representative team, you need to be doing more right from the very beginning.

Diversity in incentives:

Not every person, especially women, are attracted to roles because your company has a great nursery scheme or electric family car allowance. Consider how your benefit systems could be changed to be more inclusive, including better training incentives, or wellness programs, such as Heka. This will give you an opportunity to attract more diverse talent.

Education and awareness programs:

If we want employees to be taking cybersecurity 'seriously', we need to be tailoring communication to suit different groups, from board members to new employees, and ensuring everyone understands their role in maintaining security. The current approaches we take as an industry in bringing people along with us are not inclusive. If we want everyone to feel included and represented, we need to include and represent the different learning styles and needs of the team and users. This means regular training which should be inclusive, accessible, and possibly offered in multiple languages to cater to a diverse workforce. There are organisations that specialise in this, such as Culture Gem, and plenty of unique learning styles, such as the 'Cyber Crime Time' game.

Mentorship and career development:

Mentorship programs that support underrepresented groups are critical. It isn't possible for everyone to inherently understand everyone else's experiences, including adversities, and so offering mentors who come from diverse backgrounds and who represent underrepresented groups, makes a difference. People want to learn from those who share similar experiences and struggles. How often do we see middle-aged, white men mentoring younger women? This also filters into employee resource groups, and other community groups such as Women In Cyber Security UK. These safe spaces allow everyone to have 'someone' and meet like-minded people. It's important to really investigate what 'success' looks and feels like for different underrepresented community members and, building this into career planning, offers and advancements, not only shows consideration, but takes team members from feeling potentially unheard and unseen, to an active part of the team.

Collaborative decision-making:

Involve people from different parts of the organisation in planning and decision-making processes, including cybersecurity decision-making. When we think about 'the threat', the malicious actors themselves are more different cultures, communities, backgrounds, genders and lived experiences. To best prevent, detect and respond, the team identifying these threats must too come from different cultures, communities, backgrounds, genders and lived experiences. By doing so, you inspire thought leadership, fresh and alternative perspectives and new mindsets.

Partnerships with educational institutions:

Both organisations and individuals should be forming partnerships with schools, universities, and coding bootcamps, particularly those serving underrepresented communities, and doing their part to encourage not only cybersecurity consciousness, but new individuals to identify opportunities in STEM. These partnerships can help create pathways for students from diverse backgrounds to enter the cybersecurity field which is exactly what we need! (PS. Check out CyberFirst and STEM Ambassadors if this is a space you can help in!).

Inclusive and accessible practices:
Think before you speak and write. We must all be using inclusive language in the day to day. That could be avoiding jargon, or it could be avoiding terms which could be triggering or upsetting to individuals from different communities. Someone can be left behind, simply because the conversation has naturally excluded them. This also fits into our team training and workplace environment -we need to make sure our cybersecurity tools, resources, and training are accessible to people with disabilities and that have other reasonable adjustment needs. They deserve to be there, just as much as you.

By focusing on these strategies, an organisation can foster a more inclusive cybersecurity environment that leverages diverse perspectives for better protection against threats and fosters a culture of security awareness and responsibility. By us as individuals trying to challenge, adapt and influence these points, we show ourselves as allies and supporters, but also show ourselves to be trusted members that those from underrepresented backgrounds can talk to and lean on for support. We can then include these individuals in conversations, act as a sponsor, or advocate for them. It's one big circle, which we are all a part of.

Can you share three key lessons you have learnt that made a difference in you being successful?

We are both going to answer this as individuals. Whilst we have both had lots of similar experiences, we have also had lots of different ones, and so we want to answer this authentically as cybersecurity professionals in our own right.

Rebecca's Response:
The first key lesson I had to learn and accept, is that you just can't make everyone happy. In cybersecurity, just as in any field, it's crucial to understand that you can't please everyone. Projects often require tough decisions and prioritisation, which can sometimes lead to disagreement amongst stakeholders. Sometimes, you do have to perform above your 'rank' or have 'challenging conversations', which do get peoples backs up. Sometimes you do have to tell people their cybersecurity practices are plain shocking!

Early in my career, I learnt that whilst it's important to listen and consider the perspectives of others, you can't always be smiles and roses. It doesn't mean you're unkind-you're doing what you need to do. I also quickly learnt the need to prioritise tasks based on urgency, impact, and strategic value. Sometimes, that would mean people had to wait or didn't get what they wanted on their terms. It was driven by me. More importantly, and tied to the idea of happiness, you can't always make everyone else happy, but it's important you make yourself happy. It's essential to maintain your own mental and emotional well-being if you want to thrive. Self-care is not just a buzzword; it's a crucial aspect of performing at your best. When you prioritise yourself, you ensure that you have the resilience and clarity to handle everything else.

Lesson number two is that your role isn't your entire identity. I can't stress it enough that we are all more than our jobs. It's easy to become engrossed in the role you play at work, especially in a fast-paced, high-stakes field like cybersecurity. However, binding your entire identity to your job title or work responsibilities can be limiting and mentally exhausting. I've learned that having pursuits outside of work not only enhances personal development, but brings fresh perspectives that can be applied in professional contexts. Whether it's engaging with community service, pursuing a hobby, or enjoying time with family and friends, these activities help maintain a healthy balance, reduce burnout, and foster a broader identity beyond your professional life.

If I relate this to a lived experience, when I returned from maternity leave after my first child, my whole identity had changed, as had my working environment. This threw me into absolute turmoil and made me question if I was even worthy to work in cybersecurity. On reflection, I know for fact I am more than worthy, but that actually my identity is so much more that cybersecurity and I shouldn't have tormented myself so much. I am a Wife, a Mum, a daughter, a friend, and actually these parts of my identity are 100000% more important than my knowledge of phishing or malware families!

Another lesson I want to share is that throwing yourself into on-the-job learning, whether that be shadowing or volunteering, is worth its weight in gold. Theoretical knowledge and certifications are undoubtedly important in cybersecurity, but the real-world application of these concepts is where significant learning happens. Throughout my career, I've taken every opportunity to learn directly on the job-whether by shadowing more experienced colleagues, volunteering for new projects, or taking on challenges outside of my comfort zone. This approach has not only accelerated my learning curve, but also greatly expanded my professional network and opened up opportunities for advancement. On-the-job learning has provided me with practical, hands-on experience that is often more impactful than theoretical study alone.

I am going to be a bit cheeky and add in one final one! You don't have to follow a set career pathway. This may seem obvious, especially if you've read Chapter 5, but you do not need to have followed a set pathway, or have a STEM background to be successful in cybersecurity. I beat myself up (as such), for a long time because I felt I didn't have the cybersecurity foundations that a lot of my colleagues had, and actually even more so that my career wasn't following a set trajectory. No-one has seen a personal assistant fighting the cybersecurity fight in an Incident Command Team before! But just because it hasn't happened before, doesn't mean it shouldn't! On reflection, and as a much older, wiser cybersecurity professional, it doesn't matter! Being open to learning and simply wanting to 'do good' is what counts the most, not if you follow a set career map, or if you have a maths qualification. Bring you, your drive and ambition, and any cybersecurity team will be lucky to have you.

These lessons have not just shaped me as a professional in the cybersecurity domain, but have guided me in many other aspects of life. Embracing these have undoubtedly been pivotal in my journey. Hopefully they can help you!

Amelia's Response:
I could think of so many pieces of advice that I've been given across the course of my career, by a multitude of wonderful individuals, so trying to think of only three has been a challenge. And…having read Rebecca's answers, it's a hard act to follow!

Firstly, I would encourage you to remember that not every day is going to be your best day, and there is nothing wrong with this. We often put pressure on ourselves to perform at our highest level every single day, but the reality is that fluctuations in energy and outputs are natural. Accepting this allows you to practice self-compassion. You're less inclined to feel unnecessary frustration when things don't go as planned. Instead of seeing an off day as a failure, view it as an opportunity to recalibrate, and come back stronger. Progress isn't about perfection; it's about consistency over time, even when that means allowing yourself some grace on the tougher days.

My second piece of advice is probably an ode to my younger self. What is the rush? You don't have to rush your career. Success is not a race, and as important as it is to build your career steadily, it is equally important to take your time learning and developing. It's so easy to feel under pressure to accomplish goals as quickly as possible in a society that exalts hustle culture and overnight success stories. But experience requires time, and that's the foundation of a rewarding career. Burnout, discontent, or even the realisation that you've been following a path that doesn't really suit your beliefs and passions might result from making snap decisions in an attempt to meet external expectations. Prioritise sustainability over speed by honing your abilities to accumulate the experiences that will help you create a profession you truly love.

And finally, a key piece of advice that I've learned from my role models, you are a person before you are a professional, and so is everyone else. It's tempting to become engrossed with work titles, career expectations, and accomplishments, yet at our very core, we are all people. Your productivity does not determine your value, and it does not determine anyone else's. Beyond the job, every one of us has personal life, feelings and our own set of struggles. Accepting this can help you show others more empathy when they are struggling and more grace to yourself when you are. A happy life involves more than just moving up the corporate ladder; it also means finding balance, putting your health first, and building a meaningful life both at work and outside of it. Relationships are strengthened when you keep in mind that each coworker, manager, and client is a human being on their own journey.

I feel immensely grateful to have had such fantastic support both professionally and personally, and I sincerely believe that the balance of the two are what can make or break your success.

Chapter 9-Closing Words

We truly believe that the insights shared here can significantly revamp the way we approach careers, especially for women stepping into male-dominated fields. By now, it's clear that thriving in our careers isn't just about showing up; it's about making strategic choices. Whether it's selecting the right opportunities that spark joy and growth, or managing our time like a pro with techniques like the Eisenhower Matrix-this chapter has handed us the blueprint.

What resonates most with us, and hopefully with you too, is the emphasis on not just surviving, but genuinely thriving, by tapping into tools and mindsets that elevate our daily work and career trajectory. By setting boundaries, and occasionally saying no, we protect our time for the work that truly matters, which not only propels us forward but also safeguards our well-being.

And let's not forget the call to boost inclusivity in our spaces. It's a reminder that we all have a part to play in creating a welcoming environment, uplifting others along our own journeys. That inclusivity is more than a nice-to-have; it's a must-have for innovation and success in cybersecurity.

Navigating through this chapter feels like we're setting the scene for not just achieving success but for enjoying the ride, making the daily grind rewarding, and ensuring we're paving the way for those who follow. It's a lot to take in, but think of it as our strategic playbook-keeping us focused, efficient, and, most importantly, fulfilled in our cybersecurity careers. Let's keep this conversation going and keep pushing each other to not just reach but exceed our goals.

10 AND IF 'NONE OF THE ABOVE' APPLIES

We have delved into quite a few weeds in this book, and we're excited that you have persevered through to this chapter. We hope that you have taken ideas, knowledge and some inspiration for your next steps from this book, but we do acknowledge that some of you will have read this just to get a better view on how to be an ally, and support the women in your cybersecurity teams or community.

If this is you, we dedicate this chapter to you. You are amazing. Having strong allies that take the time to truly understand the experience of others and how they can help make the difference when it comes to the career successes and overall well-being, particularly of the women they support. We raise a glass to you, and say thank you.

Now, we'd like to bring your attention to some individuals who we think are smashing it as a 'cybersecurity ally'. Currently, this may not resonate with you, and you may really want to do more, but don't know where to start. And on the other hand, we know that there may be another bucket of people, who don't feel they should do anything, because they don't feel their contribution or efforts will actually make a difference. In this section, we will talk through what you can do, what actually helps and give you some ally inspiration.

So, before we dig in, what is allyship? Allyship is about the behaviours, practices, activities, and actions you embody to support the rights, progression, and success of a minority or marginalised group. Most importantly, it's a minority or marginalised group you yourself are not a part of, so it often involves standing up for others and even pushing for 'things' that don't directly impact you, or that you never have, or couldn't have experienced. Allyship is about empathy, consideration, caring, and speaking out. It often means taking the privilege you have to challenge the biases and conventions around you and it is most definitely a long-haul effort. All in all, an ally is bloody awesome!

If we take this to the next level, how does being an ally relate to the workplace? We are both very fortunate to have had allies throughout our careers. For us, they have been trusted individuals that are willing to listen, appreciate, and comprehend how we feel. They have taken what we have shared and reflected on their own behaviours and preconceptions, and made shifts in how they or the organisation behaves, accommodates, and works. They are people who have accepted their position or role, and that they have the ability to influence or change our environments. They have lifted us up. They are people who have educated themselves on what us, as women, needed. They have raised their own awareness, and then used that to try and educate others. They have done all this and not expected anything in return. And sometimes, they haven't even realised that they're an ally.

Being an ally is not an easy feat but it is so important. We talk for many women in cybersecurity when we say it can be lonely, and that more often than not, processes, policies, procedures, and expectancies are built by, and for the men that surround us. Right from the gender pay gap, through to gender roles influencing career opportunities. None of this will change unless we have women pushing for it, and individuals, including men and industry leadership, supporting the shift and conversation.

As promised, we want to give you some inspiration. We could have given you a plethora of allies, but in this case, we wanted to showcase just three allies, who have impacted our careers, and so we hope their words will resonate, and that you can connect with and follow them for future ideas. We hope you enjoy reading what they have to say, and that it empowers you to be a fabulous ally-however that looks for you.

Ciaran Martin

Please can you share your journey to becoming an ally for women? Was there a specific turning point or experience that inspired you to make a difference within your own career?

It isn't for me to describe myself as an ally for women, in cybersecurity or anything else. If female colleagues past and present regard me as such, then I'm very pleased. There was no major specific turning point in my career; if I had to pick out one moment, it was when a female colleague started giving me pretty blunt feedback not about the way I dealt with women, but my failure to listen enough to colleagues and to talk about myself too much. Once that happened and I started listening a bit more, I found myself (a) better at my job; and (b) overseeing the appointment of quite a few women to senior positions. When I left the NCSC, 11 of the top 20 jobs were held by women, which is pretty unusual for a cybersecurity organisation, or at least it was in 2020 when I left.

What personal qualities do you believe are essential for someone to become an effective ally?

I guess it's about one's own behaviour. After I left government, and when I was in a meeting in a new environment where I felt I had a fair degree of authority even though I wasn't chairing it, I said apologetically at the end of an overrunning discussion that I had to go because I had unbreakable school pickup commitments, and just gathered my things and walked out. I wasn't making a point - I had a child waiting for me at the school gates. But I guess being a bit older and senior I felt it was OK to do that.

To my astonishment, in the following days, three female colleagues, unprompted, got in touch with me to thank me for leading by example and helping them make the case for more disciplined meetings to help them manage their commitments. I guess it showed how much I still had to learn.

What specific actions or accountabilities do you think allies should take on to support women effectively?

This is a really tricky one. If I am honest, I have some scepticism about most of the modern management tools that are often used in this space. Excessive reliance on staff surveys was, in my experience, positively harmful if you were trying to change things. Quotas were difficult even before the DEI backlash. And bluntly, while I hope and genuinely believe I am not a Neanderthal when it comes to allyship, I absolutely am when it comes to KPIs and that sort of thing.

So what's my answer? I suppose it's something like:

- Never, ever frame the business of the whole organisation in such a way that certain groups of people, and more often than not women, feel they can't take part. In particular, check out your culture on evenings and overnight work. Neither are unavoidable, and remote access helps with working out of hours, but for the love of God do you really need a three hour (expensive) dinner to talk to someone when you could have had a coffee at 3pm? And does that away day really need to have an overnight dimension?
- Have basic rules for yourself. No 'manels'. No all- male teams.
- Watch out for problematic behaviour, especially in meetings. I don't so much mean the obvious stuff, but watching for people, often women but not always, being marginalised and never called to speak.
- Take an interest in the professional development of promising female colleagues.
- Gather feedback intelligently. There are ways of finding out whether the working environment in your team is supportive of women colleagues that are far better than HR stats and staff surveys.

But I caveat all this with humility - I am not an expert in the theory and science of the workplace, and don't claim to be.

Looking ahead, how do you see allyship evolving in the workplace? What trends or changes do you anticipate?

I hope my female friends and colleagues in the cybersecurity industry don't hate it when I say that I think our profession is making more steps forward than back. While it's very, very far from perfect, there are some good reasons for saying this. Partly, I think there are a lot of older men who are genuinely horrified at how they (we) behaved in the past, once it's been pointed out to them. Second, there are more women role models in the traditional core areas of cybersecurity, like reverse engineering malware, ethical hacking, and so on. Third, the broadening of the subject to wider disciplines like communications, risk management, governance, and so on, where there have historically been higher levels of female representation, has helped.

That said, I do worry about the wider 'culture war' in society as a whole about the workplace. The average office- whether in cybersecurity or any other discipline - is a much better environment for all than it was when I started work in the mid-1990s. Whatever the perceived 'excesses' of DEI and the backlash against it, I don't want to go back to the way things were.

What advice or encouragement would you give to others who want to become better allies for women?

Again, I am not an expert in workplace science. So, if you'll forgive me I will revert to the what many will see is a cliched response.

Every one of us men has at least one woman in our lives - a spouse, partner, sister, friend, mother - in the workplace who we want to see succeed. We would be absolutely aghast - and probably, in a macho way, furious - if they were treated in the same way as we see some of our own colleagues. So, it's pretty simple - in literally everything that you do, say, see, and respond to, imagine it's someone you deeply care about on the other end of your action.

And don't assume that everything's fine unless it's very visibly obvious that it's not. Take the time to find out.

To repeat my final caveat -these are personal reflections. I genuinely don't know how to talk and write about this. I just try to do it as best I can.

James (Jim) Wright

Please can you share your journey to becoming an ally for women? Was there a specific turning point or experience that inspired you to make a difference within your own career?

I was raised in a single parent family, where my mum had to take care of my siblings and my grandma who lived with us. She did this while maintaining a full time job, and I saw the strength she had, even in the bad times. I've always tried to support colleagues and, when possible, give people the opportunity to use their strengths regardless of who they are - recognising the value that people with different experiences, outlooks, and knowledge bring to the party. That can only make the group stronger and more effective. I also have a teenage daughter, and I want her to grow up to be able to achieve everything that she wants to without having to face barriers based on her gender.

What personal qualities do you believe are essential for someone to become an effective ally?

I've spent a lot of time learning, reading about, and trying to develop my leadership style, and I've come to believe that servant leadership is the best fit for me. This means providing support and the framework for others to achieve and become leaders in their own right while providing challenge and holding people accountable for their actions. I think this fits well with allyship as it provides a supportive and constructive atmosphere for people to be their best. I also think having a continuous learning outlook is beneficial. I am not, and never will be perfect, but I seek opportunities to challenge what I think I know, feel and believe and this has opened me up to being a good ally.

What specific actions or accountabilities do you think allies should take on to support women effectively?

I think it's important to listen and to empathise with someone with different experiences and challenges than your own - and to be open to challenge and feedback on how your actions and behaviours may impact upon others. As a leader, you have a real opportunity to role model an inclusive leadership approach, and that encourages others to speak out or hold themselves to account too. Equally, if you are lucky enough to be in a position of influence or power within an organisation, the onus is really on you to call out, report, and challenge abrasive or dismissive behaviours and set the team's culture from the top.

Looking ahead, how do you see allyship evolving in the workplace? What trends or changes do you anticipate?

I think allyship is going to be even more important in the coming years with the rise and popularity of 'masculine energy', and attacks on DEI by high-profile politicians and celebrities. Allies are going to need to be more active and vocal in supporting women in the workplace and society in general, especially where more traditional sources of support, such as HR policies, may start to fall away.

What advice or encouragement would you give to others who want to become better allies for women?

Listen and seek feedback. Be open to learning about something you cannot experience directly. Think about how a situation or behaviour would make you feel, and then look for ways to improve that experience for others.

Sam Wiltshire

Please can you share your journey to becoming an ally for women? Was there a specific turning point or experience that inspired you to make a difference within your own career?

My journey to becoming an advocate for women in technology and, in short, an ally for women started from a young age, mainly because I adore my mum, and most will say that they do. However, there was an absolute turning point, which, looking back at it now, still remains crazy to me.

I remember during one of the busiest times of my recruitment career, often the saying from hiring managers would be 'find the best man for the job Sam', or 'we want a great guy because we have a great team'. Back then something I wouldn't have taken any notice of. But there came a point when I thought to myself, why is every sentence starting with man or guy? Why can't we change that to great 'candidate, engineer, leader?' It was when I started realising this, and putting it to my clients that they also saw the stereotype that they were portraying, and they too then realised that it was time for a change. Thanks to a great bunch of clients and male allies, we were able to start making an impact within the technology space. Fast forward to today, it's not about women in technology, it is very much about allyship which encompasses it all.

What personal qualities do you believe are essential for someone to become an effective ally?

Be able to listen, take feedback and criticism, and be proactive in voicing your views.

What specific actions or accountabilities do you think allies should take on to support women effectively?

It starts with you - You've truly got to believe it, otherwise you're just being a puppet, and that's no good for you or the cause.

Be a voice. If you see something that you wouldn't do, then say something.

Surround yourself with like-minded individuals.

Lead by example - take the first step in putting things forward, calling things out, asking the question 'WHY?'

Looking ahead, how do you see allyship evolving in the workplace? What trends or changes do you anticipate?

Allyship is certainly moving in the right direction, but probably not fast enough. Something is better than nothing I suppose. I believe that it will start to have a snowball effect. I think it's only right, and it's a shame that we are in this position in the first place. However, what's encouraging to see is businesses similar to mine are starting to take the steps of employing trained professionals to help them both internally and with their offerings, which in turn then turn into conversations with their customers and actual plans are created. So, I think the trend for this year will be more workshops, and masterclasses on how to create a more equal workplace and level playing field for everyone. I believe from the data that I have seen that female talent is on the rise within the technology space which is great to see and will certainly help.

What advice or encouragement would you give to others who want to become better allies for women?

You have nothing to lose and everything to gain. Seriously - since I've started being more of an ally I've been able to make some amazing relationships with people far and wide. You'll get more than one perspective, meaning you can look at situations from multiple different viewpoints, enabling you to create solutions that solve problems. You'll be able to broaden your horizons. By learning from others, you better yourself. Bettering yourself should be your aim every day.

There is no negative to being proactive in being an ally, and for those who want to progress in their career, this will enable you to be a better leader.

Thank you to our spotlighted allies for sharing their thoughts. As we come to not only the end of this chapter, but also the end of the book, we wanted to share a story each of when allyship has truly impacted us-get a bit more personal. We hope by sharing these experiences with you, that you can see how being an ally really can be a gamechanger and really understand how 'showing up' matters.

Rebecca's story

Authentic allies can be hard to come by, and so I wanted to use this section to highlight someone special I will call Mr. R. The 'cloak and daggers' name is so that it protects his anonymity, but also if for whatever reason he reads this chapter, he knows it is him and what a difference he made. What you'll notice with the ally I share, is that he isn't a direct connection into cybersecurity, but instead part of a much wider community. Allies don't have to be in the same field, industry, country, anything. They are an individual that listens, advocates, breaks down barriers and makes change. This is what Mr. R did and still does for me.

I am a keen public speaker, and as you already know, in 2024 I was given the opportunity to deliver a TEDx talk. Now the initial reaction when I received that news was pure elation and excitement. Within a day this feeling had changed to moderate despair and panic - how will I do this? How can I do this? I have no idea what I'm doing. I'm going to make an a*** of myself. I discussed these fears with a friend, who made an introduction to a buddy of theirs, Mr R. Mr R very quickly became an ally, a friend, and someone who changed my life.

I met Mr R one sunny day in London, to have some speaker training. The purpose of the session was to help me figure out what kind of speaker I wanted to be, to get an outline for my TEDx, and just to help me get to grips with the situation I had landed myself in. I expected the session to be quite formal, structured and in essence...very 'training-esque'. My goodness, it was the opposite. We laughed, we cried, we chatted for hours. Mr R took the time to get to know me, the challenges I was facing with the talk and also dug into my self-limiting beliefs. He wanted to understand why I cared about online safety, what the current issues with explaining it were. He challenged me to think deeper and harder. He challenged me to walk away from my internalised panic and instead embrace the amazing opportunity I had at my fingertips.

You're likely reading this and thinking 'sounds wonderful, but very mentor-like'. True I guess, but I'll share what made him an ally in my eyes. For absolute months afterwards he regularly checked in and became a trusted sounding board. Whenever there was an issue with my content, he helped me break down the barriers and identify other options to make it successful. He continued to advocate for me using his own platforms and in his own communities, aiming to support my personal brand and progression. He took the doubts I had held, and bit by bit chipped away at them. At one point, I received some news on a weekend which knocked my talk wildly off course - He listened to me multiple times cry on the phone, even having to pull over on the motorway to help me strategize. He didn't have to do any of these things but he believed in me and the opportunity I had to shine.

On the TEDx day itself, Mr R was texting away to check I was ok. We didn't do last minute rehearsals or practices (he had been in receipt of a fair few draft talks and mocks so he had already been blessed with a fair few takes!) and instead focused on my wellbeing and positive headspace. He absorbed the anxieties and made me feel heard and seen. I was able to take to that red dot full of confidence and happiness -gifts he gave to me.

Mr R, I owe you so much. You helped me embrace a tumultuous time and remove the limitations. You helped me accomplish something I never would have dreamed of. You were there in the exact way I needed you to be. You did not thrust preconceptions on me, but instead helped me to tune what I had, and bosh down anything that stood in my way. You are nothing short of exceptional and I feel blessed to know you.

Amelia's story

I have been incredibly fortunate to have worked with some fantastic allies in my career, most of which, probably did not know that they were allies. It has taken me a long time to figure out what I'd like to talk about for my part of this chapter, but I think when I consider allyship, I can point out a defining moment in which I knew what allyship truly meant, and I can't honestly say it was one individual that helped, rather, a very solid group of male allies around me.

Earlier in my career, I worked in the public sector, as a very junior consultant, with a lot of responsibility. Granted, I didn't know exactly what I was doing, all of the time, but I worked in a team of three, with an amazing Security Architect and SOC Lead. I had noticed, that a member of the client team had taken quite the disliking to me, but I had brushed it off, because I may not be everyone's cup of tea, and I had made my peace with that. Now, it is worth me noting that I cannot be certain that this individual disliked me for being a woman, or being young, however, his tone towards me was notably different to others. This continued on for a few months, and I was growing frustrated, but it didn't seem like an issue, so what if he was slightly rude to me, and sent a few snotty emails? He was a client.

That was until, one day, I was having a 1-2-1 with another Security Architect on the project, who was doing an oversight role, when he saw an email on my laptop. I cannot remember the context, but I remember the tone being aggressive, and I remember feeling absolutely mortified when he asked me if this had happened before. I had to admit that this was part of a barrage of aggressive emails and general uncomfortable communications. This individual had shouted at me in a meeting that same week, and again, I'd brushed it off.

Immediately, he told me that this was not acceptable, and it should not have happened, regardless of whether he was a client or not. I didn't know it at the time, but this was a huge act of allyship. He quickly escalated this to the highest contact on the client side, who was also a fantastic support, offering several solutions from a strongly worded conversation, to a HR escalation. My line manager was informed, and he also could not have been more apologetic, and more supportive.

The key takeaway that I gathered from all of these male figures, was that they gave me autonomy. I was always asked what I wanted the outcome to be, and always reassured that I was welcome to change my mind on how I wanted to approach it, irrespective of whether processes had been kicked off already or not. That is what I believe allyship is, asking women how THEY want to be supported, not giving us support that falls below par, because you are too uncomfortable to ask.

In the months that followed, I had more support than I'd ever had before. My team completely rallied around me, and gave me opportunity, to speak up more, be bold and stand up for me as needed when engaging with this individual. Not once was I asked to step away, because I wasn't in the wrong (and we often see this being the case). I am immensely grateful for my little team for their unwavering belief in me, my imposter syndrome was through the roof, and feeling targeted by a client only made this worse.

I was able to build so much confidence and my skills grew exponentially on this project, because those around me did not let this event become a setback. Even in moments where I was under the crushing pressure of self-doubt, and the growing stress of the political landscape that impacted this specific project, I was always given empowerment, and always given the option to address problems in a way that felt authentic to me.

I'm not certain that anyone mentioned above will read this, but I'd like to hope that they know how much that meant to me, as a very junior and naïve consultant, and how much it has shaped how I advocate for others.

Chapter 10-Closing Words

Allyship to women, particularly in fields such as cybersecurity where they are underrepresented, is a critical component of fostering a diverse and inclusive environment. Throughout this chapter, we have explored the multifaceted role of an ally, and how their support can catalyse significant changes in both individual careers and broader organisational cultures. The stories and strategies highlighted have demonstrated that being an ally means more than just passive support-it requires proactive engagement, continuous learning, and a commitment to challenge the status quo.

Effective allyship involves recognising the unique challenges faced by women in the workplace, and taking concrete actions to address these challenges, even when they may not directly affect you. It encompasses everything from listening and understanding, to advocating and amplifying women's voices, creating opportunities for growth, and enforcing equitable practices. Above all, allyship is about leveraging one's own position of privilege to engineer change that promotes fairness and equality.

As we conclude this chapter, remember that the journey of allyship is ongoing and ever-evolving. It is a commitment to stand alongside women, not just in moments of overt discrimination, but every day, within the nuanced dynamics of professional environments. Each of us has the power to make a difference. Whether you are just beginning to understand what it means to be an ally, or are well on your way to advocating for gender diversity and equity, your efforts are vital and valued.

Let us carry forward the inspiration from the outstanding allies profiled in this chapter and strive to incorporate those lessons into our daily lives. By fostering an atmosphere where allyship is not just encouraged but expected, we can collectively work towards a world where gender no longer dictates ones opportunities or outcomes in cybersecurity or any other field. Thank you for dedicating time to become more informed and responsive to this crucial issue.

Together, let's continue to support, empower, and champion the women in our professional circles and beyond, forging pathways toward truly inclusive and equitable workplaces.

Thank you and Goodbye!

It has been nothing short of amazing to write this book. We have had to dig deep, go on a rollercoaster of feelings, and relive a lot of memories, but all for the purpose of creating an authentic, relatable piece of text which we hope you can embrace. In this book, we have covered so many topics, from mentorship to facing adversity head on. We have even shared some of the exceptional and inspiring individuals we have met on our own journeys. We know you may not resonate with every element of the book, but we do hope you have found solace in some of our stories and in knowing that in one way or another, you are not alone.

We do want to end this book by really stressing the importance of not being alone. There is a huge community out there, but it is for you to drive and make those connections. Whether it's a colleague or contact in an interest group, networking at an event, or attending a conference, please put out the feelers and embrace those meaningful relationships. It can take you from loneliness to absolute joy. There is nothing like knowing you have just even one friend, who gets how you're feeling and what you're going through. Be bold and make that connection.

We also appreciate, that some of the questions and answers in this book could be triggering and could bring up an awful lot of feelings. You could be in the heat of a horrible situation, be struggling or be low. If this is you, whilst we hope the book has helped summon some strength and hope, it is so important to seek help, whether that be via your GP, Medical Practitioner or via a helpline or therapist (note the list of resources at the front of this book). Your mental health and wellbeing are critical. They are what matters the absolute most, so please do what you need to do to be happy and well. This book will be waiting for you, as will we, when you're ready to continue down the career path again.

So, where do we go now? In terms of the book, let it forever more be a guide and resource. It is here and can empower you to drive your own cybersecurity journeys. We only ask you help us out, by sharing the book far and wide. We want to reach as many woman as possible and get these critical messages and life lessons out there. So, lend your copy to a buddy, share it with your mentee, write about is on LinkedIn and use the tag #cyberagonyaunts. We are loud, proud, and here for you all. Let's bring as many women on the journey with us as possible.

This all being said; we do recognise that many of the questions and associated experiences we have shared will resonate beyond the boundaries of professionals in cybersecurity and even beyond gender. Self-doubt, anxiety, workplace bias can impact anyone at any point regardless of their career or lifestyle choices. Whilst you may have picked this book as a woman wanting a career in a predominantly male dominated field, such as cybersecurity, know you can take the lessons learned beyond that and into your life. Use it to support your friends, and fellow women to demonstrate allyship...there is something for everyone to take.

In terms of us as writers and individuals, we aren't sure what will happen next. Cybersecurity is a big old space and we have so much more to achieve, both in our careers and beyond. We want to keep making a difference, and supporting both organisations and individuals alike to make cybersecurity conscious choices. We do know, this writing experience has brought up closer than ever, and for that we will eternally be grateful.

We send you so much love and luck for your next steps whatever they may be. We are proud of you for reading and engaging with our book, and hope you can go on to have a meaningful and empowering career in your field of choice, and in a way that makes you shine. Keep smiling, keep pushing, and never forget how amazing you are.

Love & light,

Rebecca & Amelia x

A DEDICATION - AALIA MAHOMED

Aalia Mahomed was a beacon of intelligence and determination. Her love, humour and ambition shone, inspiring all who knew her. She was taken far too soon. She will always be missed, cherished and loved.

We honour Aalia's memory by committing to mentor and support girls and women in STEM careers, nurture their talents, and help them achieve their dreams just as she had hoped to achieve hers. Her legacy is not just in the memories we hold dear, but in our commitment to create a more inclusive and supportive environment for women in the industry.

'Indeed, we belong to Allah, and indeed to Him we will return.'
Quran 2:156

Aalia, your light will forever guide us.

Love always xxx

Question Guide

Sam Wiltshire Pg 155

Authors

Rebecca Taylor - https://www.linkedin.com/in/rebecca-taylor-2646ab22/

Amelia Hewitt - https://www.linkedin.com/in/amelia-hewitt-44b510182/

Contact us at cyberagonyaunts@gmail.com

Contributions – Role Models

Laura Reilly- https://www.linkedin.com/in/laura-reilly-marketing-social-media/

Radhika Modha- https://uk.linkedin.com/in/radhikamodha

Emma Mackenzie- https://www.linkedin.com/emmasmmackenzie

Bharti Lim- https://www.linkedin.com/in/bhartilim/

Rafat Yewande Alabelewe- https://www.linkedin.com/in/rafatalabelewe

Sophie Powell- https://www.linkedin.com/in/sophie--powell/

Bronwyn Boyle- https://www.linkedin.com/in/bronwynboyle/

Contributors- Allies

Sam Wiltshire- https://www.linkedin.com/in/sam-wiltshire-uk/

James (Jim) Wright- www.linkedin.com/in/james-wright-13810052

Ciaran Martin- ciaranm@bsky.social

Organisations

Hewitt Partnerships- https://hewittpartnershipsltd.com/

CybAid - https://cybaid.co.uk/

Events

TEDxWalthamstow- https://www.youtube.com/watch?v=VyfhkfE3nHA

Bharti Lim TEDx- https://www.youtube.com/watch?v=qbhj33nsQBk

References

Cambridge Dictionary (2025). *challenge.* [online] Available at: https://dictionary.cambridge.org/us/dictionary/english/challenge.

Clear, J. (2014). *How to be More Productive by Using the 'Eisenhower Box'.* [online] James Clear. Available at: https://jamesclear.com/eisenhower-box.

Cuncic, A. (2022). *Imposter Syndrome: Why You May Feel Like a Fraud.* [online] Verywell Mind. Available at: https://www.verywellmind.com/imposter-syndrome-and-social-anxiety-disorder-4156469.

Endometriosis UK (2019). *Endometriosis UK | the leading UK charity that supports women living with endometriosis.* [online] Endometriosis-uk.org. Available at: https://www.endometriosis-uk.org/.

Equality Act (2010). *Equality Act 2010.* [online] Legislation.gov.uk. Available at: https://www.legislation.gov.uk/ukpga/2010/15/contents.

Granovetter, M. (1983). *The Strength of Weak Ties: A Network Theory Revisited. Sociological Theory,* [online] 1(6), pp.201–233. Available at: doi:https://doi.org/10.2307/202051.

Holdsworth, J. (2023). *AI bias.* [online] Ibm.com. Available at: https://www.ibm.com/think/topics/ai-bias.

Impostor Syndrome Institute. (n.d.). *Rethinking Impostor Syndrome.* [online] Available at: https://impostorsyndrome.com/rethinking-impostor-syndrome/.

McArdle, T. (2023). *Read the powerful 'Barbie' monologue about being a woman that America Ferrera performed '30 to 50' times.* [online] Peoplemag. Available at: https://people.com/read-the-powerful-barbie-monologue-about-being-a-woman-that-america-ferrera-performed-30-to-50-times-7565806.

Medium (2019). *Welcome to Medium, where words matter.* [online] Medium.com.

Available at: https://medium.com/about.

Mental Health UK (2024). *Burnout.* [online] Mental Health UK. Available at: https://mentalhealth-uk.org/burnout/

Microsoft.com. (2024). *Online Training – Learn New Technology Skills | Microsoft.* [online] Available at: https://www.microsoft.com/en-us/microsoft-learn?msockid=2110ec4f8e946fb133c0f81a8f816ea1.

Mitre.org. (2015). *ATT&CK Training | MITRE ATT&CK®.* [online] Available at: https://attack.mitre.org/resources/learn-more-about-attack/training/

NHS (2021). *Get Your Mind Plan - Every Mind Matters.* [online] nhs.uk. Available at: https://www.nhs.uk/every-mind-matters/mental-wellbeing-tips/your-mind-plan-quiz/.

Ro, C. (2019). *Dunbar's number: Why we can only maintain 150 relationships.* [online] bbc.com. Available at: https://www.bbc.com/future/article/20191001-dunbars-number-why-we-can-only-maintain-150-relationships.

Tech, in (2024). *MotherBoard.* [online] MotherBoard. Available at: https://motherboardmovement.co.uk/community/reality-of-mums-in-tech-results

UK Cyber Security Council. (2023). *Professional Registration.* [online] Available at: https://www.ukcybersecuritycouncil.org.uk/professional-registration/

UK Cyber Security Council. (2023). *Cyber security careers: a route map through the 16 cyber security specialisms.* [online] Available at: https://www.ukcybersecuritycouncil.org.uk/careers-and-learning/cyber-career-framework/

Yoana Karamitrova (2022). *20 Powerful Networking Questions To Ask When The Conversation Is Stuck.* [online] Elegant Mind. Available at: https://www.elegantmind.co.uk/networking-questions-to-ask/

Resources

Amazon.co.uk. (2025). *The Personal Branding Playbook: Turn Your Personality Into Your Competitive Advantage eBook : Sordell, Amelia: Amazon.co.uk: Kindle Store.* [online] Available at: https://www.amazon.co.uk/Personal-Branding-Playbook-Personality-Competitive-ebook/dp/B0DQ9HYSS4?ref_=ast_author_mpb

Cybrary (2019). *Free Cyber Security Training and Career Development | Cybrary.* [online] Cybrary. Available at: https://www.cybrary.it/.

Empowering You (2025). *Empowering You Home.* [online] Available at: https://www.empowering-you.co.uk/

FIRST - *Forum of Incident Response and Security Teams. (2015). Women of FIRST SIG.* [online] Available at: https://www.first.org/global/sigs/wof/

FutureLearn (2023). *Free Online Courses - FutureLearn.* [online] FutureLearn. Available at: https://www.futurelearn.com/.

Linkedin.com. (2025). *Hacker in Heels | LinkedIn.* [online] Available at: https://www.linkedin.com/company/hackerinheels

LinkedIn (2019). *Introducing LinkedIn Learning, personalized eLearning for your organization.* [online] Linkedin.com. Available at: https://learning.linkedin.com/.

Linkedin.com. (2023). *LMF NETWORK (Like Minded Females) | LinkedIn.* [online] Available at: https://www.linkedin.com/company/like-minded-females/

Linkedin.com. (2025). *Women + Cybersecurity = Women's Society of Cyberjutsu | LinkedIn.* [online] Available at: https://www.linkedin.com/company/women-s-society-of-cyberjutsu

MotherBoard (2025). *MotherBoard.* [online] MotherBoard. Available at: https://motherboardmovement.co.uk/

WiCyS UK&I Affiliate (2024). *WiCyS UK&I Affiliate.* [online] Google.com. Available at: https://sites.google.com/wicys.org/wicysuk

Halzak (2025). *Halzak* online] Google.com. Available at: https://halzak.com/

***Photography Credit*:** @photographybyevangelina (Instagram)

Photos in the role model and allyship sections of this book were self-provided by individual contributors.

Cover Credit: *Harry Hewitt*

ABOUT THE AUTHORS

Amelia serves as the Director of Hewitt Partnerships Ltd, a Governance, Risk Management, and Compliance (GRC) Cyber Advisory, and is the Founder of CybAid. Rebecca is a Threat Intelligence Knowledge Manager and Researcher in the Counter Threat Unit at Secureworks, a Sophos company. They combine both their expertise of the Cyber industry with their shared experiences of being female professionals to provide their 'Agony Aunt'-style advice to those both seasoned and aspiring within the world of Cyber.